Author Journey

Weekly Planner & Success Guide

LAURIE J. EDWARDS & DEMI STEVENS

Copyright © 2020 Laurie J. Edwards & Demi Stevens

All Rights Reserved

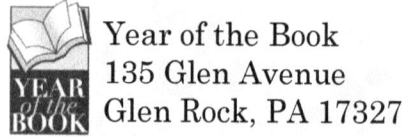
Year of the Book
135 Glen Avenue
Glen Rock, PA 17327

Print ISBN: 978-1-64649-077-6

All rights reserved. No portion of this book may be reproduced in any form without permission from the publisher, except as permitted by U.S. copyright law. For permissions contact publisher at the address above.

Welcome

As writers, we're often told, "Write the book you wish were in the world," and for Laurie and Demi, that's a day planner to organize and guide our writing and publishing productivity, our habits for success, reminders to not take ourselves so seriously, and of course, to inspire and fill the creative well.

*"Breathe, darling. This is just a chapter.
It's not your whole story." —S.C. Lourie*

Friends often ask how we get so much done, so together we set about a review of our previous year in business and life. This book is a result of the lessons we learned.

As we thumbed the pages of our well-worn datebooks, it became obvious that—like everyone else—we had forgotten much of what seemed like a big deal at the time. The day-to-day drifted away, and even the sparkling points we ought to have celebrated vigorously became just one more checkmark that let us start the next task on our to-do list.

*If you don't want to burn out,
stop living like you're on fire.*

By reviewing the previous 12 months in depth, we discovered things about the way we spent our time and the way those tasks had been rewarded (monetarily, physically, and emotionally). Now, you'd think we might have understood this intuitively. Because, after all, we were the ones living it. But in the moment, it's difficult to notice the water warming around you one degree at a time. Until it's boiling.

We longed for a way forward without forgetting these hard-won insights. And we hope you'll benefit, too, because writers are a beautiful breed of humans, and we want to see you thrive. Your words have power. Your stories need to be shared. And together, we can change the world.

*"You can't go back and change the beginning,
but you can start where you are
and change the ending." —C.S. Lewis*

Looking Back... and Looking Ahead

To launch you into your best and most rewarding writing year, it's important to acknowledge and give gratitude for the year that came before. In the pages that follow, consider each question, and WRITE your responses in PEN. It's time for you to stop playing small. Perfection does not serve you. Just dive in and get messy. Your life is a first draft!

Take time to celebrate the milestones achieved this past year and recognize goals left undone. You get to decide which ones move forward with you. If a long-held goal or belief no longer serves you, then thank and release it. You'll need space in which to create.

By selectively saying 'no' to tasks that don't feed you, you can finally find a way to say 'yes' to your dreams.

A writer's journey begins with ONE STEP. You took your first step forward by sitting down with this planner. Where do you go next? That's up to YOU.

Where do YOU want to be this time next year?

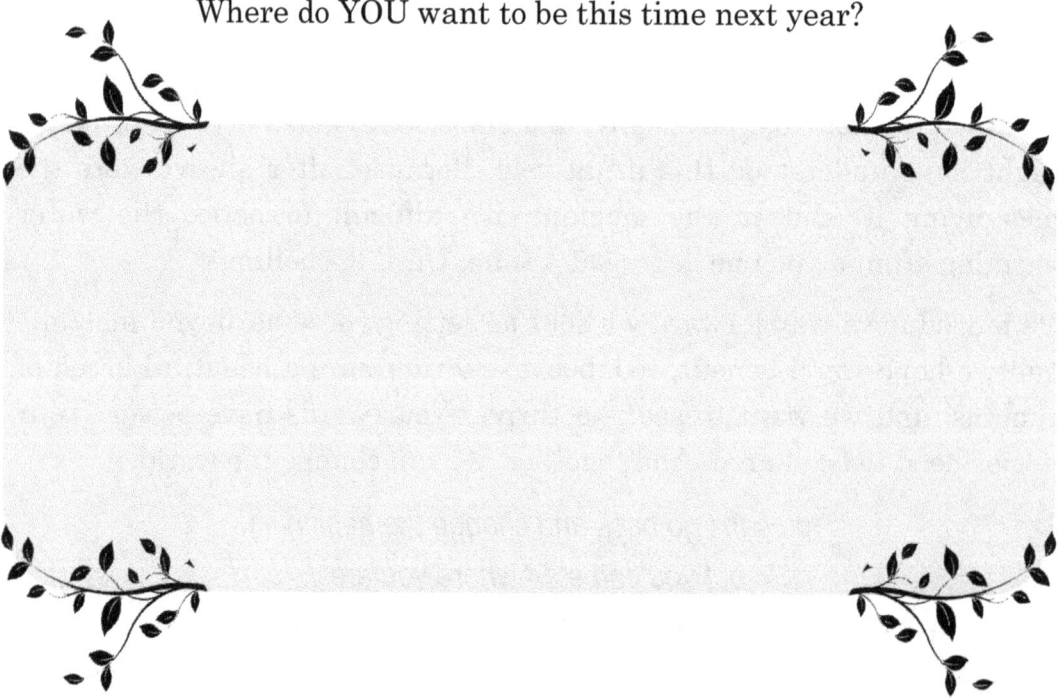

Don't let life sidetrack you from reaching YOUR goals. Use this planner as a roadmap for all your HOPES and DREAMS. Make the book yours. Write in it. Plan in it. Live an INSPIRED life.

- Envision your future
- Decide on your goals
- Set daily intentions
- Track writing progress
- Overcome procrastination
- Evaluate your progress
- Take time for gratitude
- Remember appointments
- Record story ideas
- Check off books you read
- Organize writing contacts
- List expenses and submissions
- Note your accomplishments
- Use time wisely

"When there is too much, something is missing." —Leo Rosten

Think of one word to describe your IDEAL year:

Now it's time for a little review.

Looking Back...

What were the most memorable moments of last year?

What am I most grateful for?

What do I wish I'd done less of?

What were my top successes for the year?

Am I happy with my priorities?

How do I feel about my writing/life balance?

How am I different from this time last year?

Am I happy with my progress this year?

What would I like to change?

**What were my greatest challenges?
What did I learn from them?**

Who inspired me most this year? How and why?

What are the top three things I wish I'd accomplished?

BE SURE TO INCLUDE THESE AS PRIORITIES IN PLANNING THIS YEAR.

Looking Ahead...

As the new year opens before me, what steps can I take to reach my dreams? Begin by moving beyond the POSSIBLE to envisioning the INCREDIBLE.

If there are NO LIMITS and ANYTHING is POSSIBLE, I'd...

Use the next page to map the biggest goals you want to achieve in each area of your life:

* Personal
* Family
* Writing
* Business
* Health
* Spiritual

Draw connecting lines from each goal to the steps you'll take to get it done.

Ex:

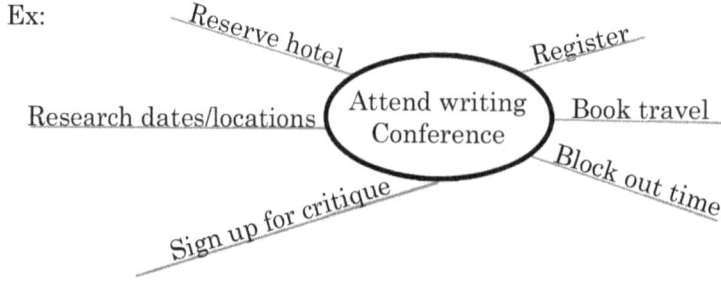

My Creative Space

Mindmap. Sketch. List. Color.
Use whatever stimulates you to record your plans and goals.
Create a vision that inspires you, a purpose that makes you passionate to start each day.

Select the dream that resonates most with you and put it on the tree trunk. Then break down the dream into goals as follows:

SOIL: What support or resources do you need to make this happen? List mentors, books, classes, etc. Maybe you need more time, money, office space. Try to come up with ways to get the support you need.

ROOTS: The roots are your core beliefs. They underpin any dream. What do you believe about yourself and your ability to suceed? If your core beliefs need to be changed, write new, empowering beliefs you plan to adopt this year.

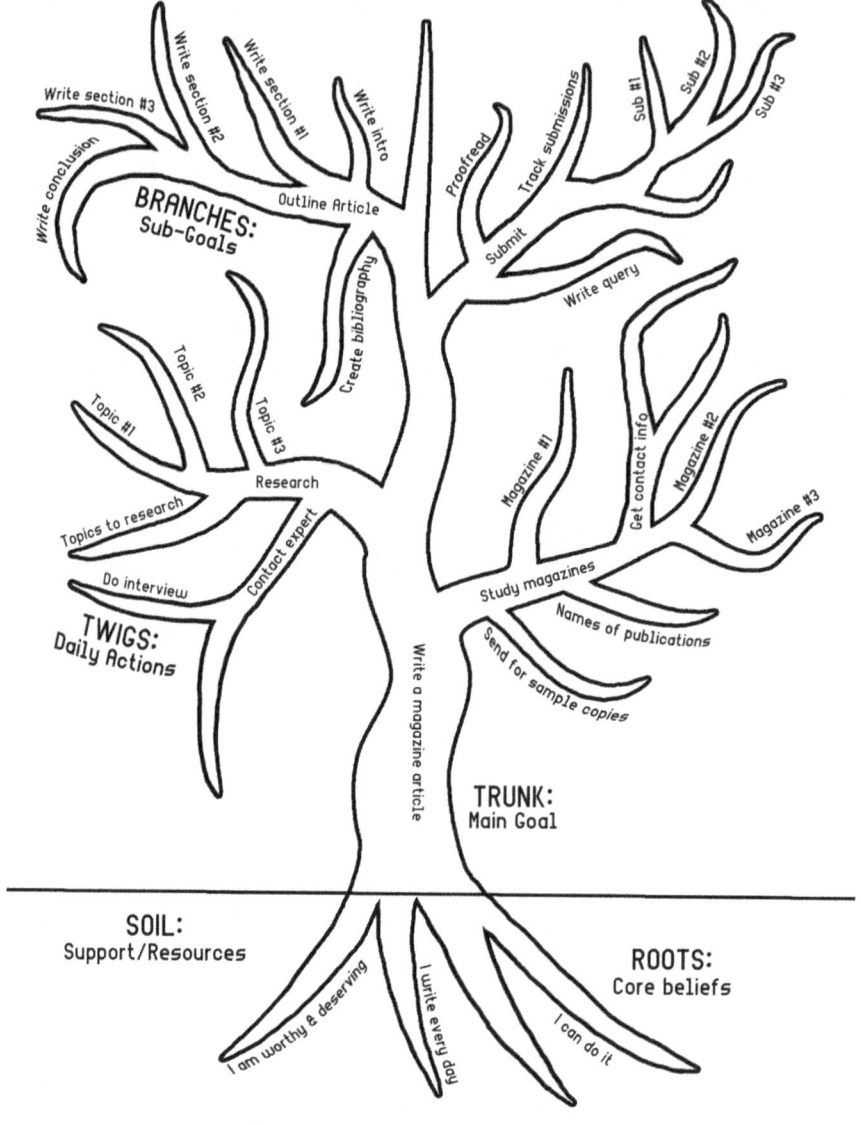

BRANCHES: Break down the goal to doable actions.

TWIGS: Use these for smaller actions or daily goals. Add deadlines if desired.

LEAVES: When you complete a goal, draw a leaf on the end of that branch. Date it and color it in. When you've completed all your goals, you'll have a flowering tree. Make copies of the tree for other goals.

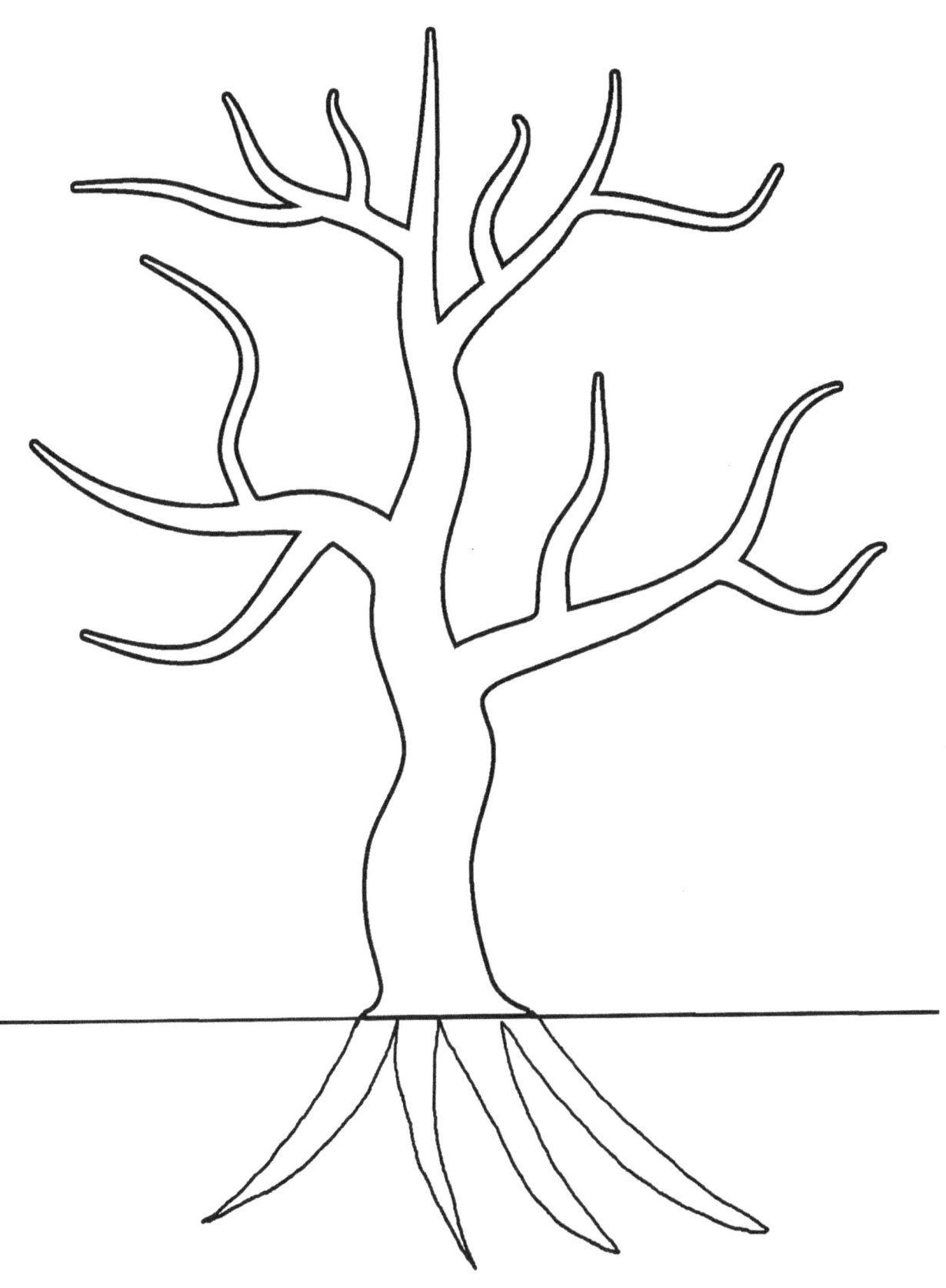

Need more space to map out your awesome dream goals?
Visit YOTBpress.com/authorjourney for free printables!

Dream Goals

Make a list of everything you've been wanting to do. Revisit this list each month, and add items to your calendar...because making time for your goals is the only way to get them DONE

- [x] 1. Plan for the writing year ahead
- [ ] 2.
- [ ] 3.
- [ ] 4.
- [ ] 5.
- [ ] 6.
- [ ] 7.
- [ ] 8.
- [ ] 9.
- [ ] 10.
- [ ] 11.
- [ ] 12.
- [ ] 13.
- [ ] 14.
- [ ] 15.
- [ ] 16.
- [ ] 17.
- [ ] 18.
- [ ] 19.
- [ ] 20.
- [ ] 21.
- [ ] 22.

- [ ] 23. _____
- [ ] 24. _____
- [ ] 25. _____
- [ ] 26. _____
- [ ] 27. _____
- [ ] 28. _____
- [ ] 29. _____
- [ ] 30. _____
- [ ] 31. _____
- [ ] 32. _____
- [ ] 33. _____
- [ ] 34. _____
- [ ] 35. _____
- [ ] 36. _____
- [ ] 37. _____
- [ ] 38. _____
- [ ] 39. _____
- [ ] 40. _____
- [ ] 41. _____
- [ ] 42. _____
- [ ] 43. _____
- [ ] 44. _____
- [ ] 45. _____

Need more space to list your awesome dream goals?

Visit YOTBpress.com/authorjourney for free printables!

2020

~ January ~
S	M	T	W	T	F	S
			1	2	3	4
5	6	7	8	9	10	11
12	13	14	15	16	17	18
19	20	21	22	23	24	25
26	27	28	29	30	31	

~ February ~
S	M	T	W	T	F	S
						1
2	3	4	5	6	7	8
9	10	11	12	13	14	15
16	17	18	19	20	21	22
23	24	25	26	27	28	29

~ March ~
S	M	T	W	T	F	S
1	2	3	4	5	6	7
8	9	10	11	12	13	14
15	16	17	18	19	20	21
22	23	24	25	26	27	28
29	30	31				

~ April ~
S	M	T	W	T	F	S
			1	2	3	4
5	6	7	8	9	10	11
12	13	14	15	16	17	18
19	20	21	22	23	24	25
26	27	28	29	30		

~ May ~
S	M	T	W	T	F	S
					1	2
3	4	5	6	7	8	9
10	11	12	13	14	15	16
17	18	19	20	21	22	23
24	25	26	27	28	29	30
31						

~ June ~
S	M	T	W	T	F	S
	1	2	3	4	5	6
7	8	9	10	11	12	13
14	15	16	17	18	19	20
21	22	23	24	25	26	27
28	29	30				

~ July ~
S	M	T	W	T	F	S
			1	2	3	4
5	6	7	8	9	10	11
12	13	14	15	16	17	18
19	20	21	22	23	24	25
26	27	28	29	30	31	

~ August ~
S	M	T	W	T	F	S
						1
2	3	4	5	6	7	8
9	10	11	12	13	14	15
16	17	18	19	20	21	22
23	24	25	26	27	28	29
30	31					

~ September ~
S	M	T	W	T	F	S
		1	2	3	4	5
6	7	8	9	10	11	12
13	14	15	16	17	18	19
20	21	22	23	24	25	26
27	28	29	30			

~ October ~
S	M	T	W	T	F	S
				1	2	3
4	5	6	7	8	9	10
11	12	13	14	15	16	17
18	19	20	21	22	23	24
25	26	27	28	29	30	31

~ November ~
S	M	T	W	T	F	S
1	2	3	4	5	6	7
8	9	10	11	12	13	14
15	16	17	18	19	20	21
22	23	24	25	26	27	28
29	30					

~ December ~
S	M	T	W	T	F	S
		1	2	3	4	5
6	7	8	9	10	11	12
13	14	15	16	17	18	19
20	21	22	23	24	25	26
27	28	29	30	31		

Holidays

Jan 1	New Year's Day	Jul 3	Independence Day (obs.)
Jan 20	MLK Jr. Day	Jul 4	Independence Day
Feb 14	Valentine's Day	Sep 7	Labor Day
Feb 17	Presidents' Day	Sep 18	Rosh Hashanah
Mar 17	St. Patrick's Day	Sep 27	Yom Kippur
Apr 12	Easter	Oct 12	Columbus Day
May 25	Memorial Day	Oct 31	Halloween
Nov 11	Veterans Day		
Nov 26	Thanksgiving Day		
Dec 10	Hanukkah Begins		
Dec 24	Christmas Eve		
Dec 25	Christmas Day		
Dec 31	New Year's Eve		

2021

~ January ~

S	M	T	W	T	F	S
					1	2
3	4	5	6	7	8	9
10	11	12	13	14	15	16
17	18	19	20	21	22	23
24	25	26	27	28	29	30
31						

~ February ~

S	M	T	W	T	F	S
	1	2	3	4	5	6
7	8	9	10	11	12	13
14	15	16	17	18	19	20
21	22	23	24	25	26	27
28						

~ March ~

S	M	T	W	T	F	S
	1	2	3	4	5	6
7	8	9	10	11	12	13
14	15	16	17	18	19	20
21	22	23	24	25	26	27
28	29	30	31			

~ April ~

S	M	T	W	T	F	S
				1	2	3
4	5	6	7	8	9	10
11	12	13	14	15	16	17
18	19	20	21	22	23	24
25	26	27	28	29	30	

~ May ~

S	M	T	W	T	F	S
						1
2	3	4	5	6	7	8
9	10	11	12	13	14	15
16	17	18	19	20	21	22
23	24	25	26	27	28	29
30	31					

~ June ~

S	M	T	W	T	F	S
		1	2	3	4	5
6	7	8	9	10	11	12
13	14	15	16	17	18	19
20	21	22	23	24	25	26
27	28	29	30			

~ July ~

S	M	T	W	T	F	S
				1	2	3
4	5	6	7	8	9	10
11	12	13	14	15	16	17
18	19	20	21	22	23	24
25	26	27	28	29	30	31

~ August ~

S	M	T	W	T	F	S
1	2	3	4	5	6	7
8	9	10	11	12	13	14
15	16	17	18	19	20	21
22	23	24	25	26	27	28
29	30					

~ September ~

S	M	T	W	T	F	S
			1	2	3	4
5	6	7	8	9	10	11
12	13	14	15	16	17	18
19	20	21	22	23	24	25
26	27	28	29	30		

~ October ~

S	M	T	W	T	F	S
					1	2
3	4	5	6	7	8	9
10	11	12	13	14	15	16
17	18	19	20	21	22	23
24	25	26	27	28	29	30
31						

~ November ~

S	M	T	W	T	F	S
	1	2	3	4	5	6
7	8	9	10	11	12	13
14	15	16	17	18	19	20
21	22	23	24	25	26	27
28	29	30				

~ December ~

S	M	T	W	T	F	S
			1	2	3	4
5	6	7	8	9	10	11
12	13	14	15	16	17	18
19	20	21	22	23	24	25
26	27	28	29	30		

Holidays

Jan 1	New Year's Day
Jan 18	MLK Jr. Day
Feb 14	Valentine's Day
Feb 15	Presidents' Day
Mar 17	St. Patrick's Day
Apr 4	Easter
May 31	Memorial Day
Jul 4	Independence Day
Jul 5	Independence Day (obs.)
Sep 6	Labor Day
Sep 6	Rosh Hashanah
Sep 15	Yom Kippur
Oct 11	Columbus Day
Oct 31	Halloween
Nov 11	Veterans Day
Nov 25	Thanksgiving Day
Nov 28	Hanukkah Begins
Dec 24	Christmas Eve
Dec 25	Christmas Day
Dec 31	New Year's Eve

Month:

MONDAY	TUESDAY	WEDNESDAY

This Month's Focus

Social Media Goals

THURSDAY	FRIDAY	SATURDAY	SUNDAY

 Sales / Releases / Queries

Week Of

"A goal is a dream with a deadline."
—Napoleon Hill

PRIORITY GOALS

TO DO

DREAM GOALS

	MONDAY		TUESDAY		WEDNESDAY
	INTENTIONS		INTENTIONS		INTENTIONS
6:00		6:00		6:00	
6:30		6:30		6:30	
7:00		7:00		7:00	
7:30		7:30		7:30	
8:00		8:00		8:00	
8:30		8:30		8:30	
9:00		9:00		9:00	
9:30		9:30		9:30	
10:00		10:00		10:00	
10:30		10:30		10:30	
11:00		11:00		11:00	
11:30		11:30		11:30	
	I AM CREATIVE		MY WORDS MATTER		LIFE IS GOOD
12:00		12:00		12:00	
12:30		12:30		12:30	
1:00		1:00		1:00	
1:30		1:30		1:30	
2:00		2:00		2:00	
2:30		2:30		2:30	
3:00		3:00		3:00	
3:30		3:30		3:30	
4:00		4:00		4:00	
4:30		4:30		4:30	
5:00		5:00		5:00	
5:30		5:30		5:30	
6:00		6:00		6:00	
6:30		6:30		6:30	
7:00		7:00		7:00	
7:30		7:30		7:30	
8:00		8:00		8:00	
WRITING PROGRESS		WRITING PROGRESS		WRITING PROGRESS	
GRATITUDES					

THURSDAY	FRIDAY	SATURDAY	SUNDAY
INTENTIONS	INTENTIONS	INTENTIONS	INTENTIONS
6:00	6:00	6:00	6:00
6:30	6:30	6:30	6:30
7:00	7:00	7:00	7:00
7:30	7:30	7:30	7:30
8:00	8:00	8:00	8:00
8:30	8:30	8:30	8:30
9:00	9:00	9:00	9:00
9:30	9:30	9:30	9:30
10:00	10:00	10:00	10:00
10:30	10:30	10:30	10:30
11:00	11:00	11:00	11:00
11:30	11:30	11:30	11:30
I MEET MY GOALS	BUILDING MY DREAMS	NO EXCUSES	I AM AN AUTHOR
12:00	12:00	12:00	12:00
12:30	12:30	12:30	12:30
1:00	1:00	1:00	1:00
1:30	1:30	1:30	1:30
2:00	2:00	2:00	2:00
2:30	2:30	2:30	2:30
3:00	3:00	3:00	3:00
3:30	3:30	3:30	3:30
4:00	4:00	4:00	4:00
4:30	4:30	4:30	4:30
5:00	5:00	5:00	5:00
5:30	5:30	5:30	5:30
6:00	6:00	6:00	6:00
6:30	6:30	6:30	6:30
7:00	7:00	7:00	7:00
7:30	7:30	7:30	7:30
8:00	8:00	8:00	8:00
WRITING PROGRESS	WRITING PROGRESS	WRITING PROGRESS	WRITING PROGRESS

LOOKING AHEAD

Week Of

"Write a short story every week. It's not possible to write 52 bad short stories in a row."
—Ray Bradbury

PRIORITY GOALS

TO DO

DREAM GOALS

	MONDAY		TUESDAY		WEDNESDAY
	INTENTIONS		INTENTIONS		INTENTIONS
6:00		6:00		6:00	
6:30		6:30		6:30	
7:00		7:00		7:00	
7:30		7:30		7:30	
8:00		8:00		8:00	
8:30		8:30		8:30	
9:00		9:00		9:00	
9:30		9:30		9:30	
10:00		10:00		10:00	
10:30		10:30		10:30	
11:00		11:00		11:00	
11:30		11:30		11:30	
	I AM CREATIVE		MY WORDS MATTER		LIFE IS GOOD
12:00		12:00		12:00	
12:30		12:30		12:30	
1:00		1:00		1:00	
1:30		1:30		1:30	
2:00		2:00		2:00	
2:30		2:30		2:30	
3:00		3:00		3:00	
3:30		3:30		3:30	
4:00		4:00		4:00	
4:30		4:30		4:30	
5:00		5:00		5:00	
5:30		5:30		5:30	
6:00		6:00		6:00	
6:30		6:30		6:30	
7:00		7:00		7:00	
7:30		7:30		7:30	
8:00		8:00		8:00	
WRITING PROGRESS		WRITING PROGRESS		WRITING PROGRESS	
GRATITUDES					

THURSDAY		FRIDAY		SATURDAY		SUNDAY	
INTENTIONS		INTENTIONS		INTENTIONS		INTENTIONS	
6:00		6:00		6:00		6:00	
6:30		6:30		6:30		6:30	
7:00		7:00		7:00		7:00	
7:30		7:30		7:30		7:30	
8:00		8:00		8:00		8:00	
8:30		8:30		8:30		8:30	
9:00		9:00		9:00		9:00	
9:30		9:30		9:30		9:30	
10:00		10:00		10:00		10:00	
10:30		10:30		10:30		10:30	
11:00		11:00		11:00		11:00	
11:30		11:30		11:30		11:30	
	I MEET MY GOALS		BUILDING MY DREAMS		NO EXCUSES		I AM AN AUTHOR
12:00		12:00		12:00		12:00	
12:30		12:30		12:30		12:30	
1:00		1:00		1:00		1:00	
1:30		1:30		1:30		1:30	
2:00		2:00		2:00		2:00	
2:30		2:30		2:30		2:30	
3:00		3:00		3:00		3:00	
3:30		3:30		3:30		3:30	
4:00		4:00		4:00		4:00	
4:30		4:30		4:30		4:30	
5:00		5:00		5:00		5:00	
5:30		5:30		5:30		5:30	
6:00		6:00		6:00		6:00	
6:30		6:30		6:30		6:30	
7:00		7:00		7:00		7:00	
7:30		7:30		7:30		7:30	
8:00		8:00		8:00		8:00	
WRITING PROGRESS		WRITING PROGRESS		WRITING PROGRESS		WRITING PROGRESS	

LOOKING AHEAD

Week Of

"We do not need magic to change the world. We carry all the power we need inside ourselves already.
—Joanne Rowling

PRIORITY GOALS

TO DO

DREAM GOALS

	MONDAY		TUESDAY		WEDNESDAY
	INTENTIONS		INTENTIONS		INTENTIONS
6:00		6:00		6:00	
6:30		6:30		6:30	
7:00		7:00		7:00	
7:30		7:30		7:30	
8:00		8:00		8:00	
8:30		8:30		8:30	
9:00		9:00		9:00	
9:30		9:30		9:30	
10:00		10:00		10:00	
10:30		10:30		10:30	
11:00		11:00		11:00	
11:30		11:30		11:30	
	I AM CREATIVE		MY WORDS MATTER		LIFE IS GOOD
12:00		12:00		12:00	
12:30		12:30		12:30	
1:00		1:00		1:00	
1:30		1:30		1:30	
2:00		2:00		2:00	
2:30		2:30		2:30	
3:00		3:00		3:00	
3:30		3:30		3:30	
4:00		4:00		4:00	
4:30		4:30		4:30	
5:00		5:00		5:00	
5:30		5:30		5:30	
6:00		6:00		6:00	
6:30		6:30		6:30	
7:00		7:00		7:00	
7:30		7:30		7:30	
8:00		8:00		8:00	
WRITING PROGRESS		WRITING PROGRESS		WRITING PROGRESS	
GRATITUDES					

THURSDAY		FRIDAY		SATURDAY		SUNDAY	
INTENTIONS		INTENTIONS		INTENTIONS		INTENTIONS	
6:00		6:00		6:00		6:00	
6:30		6:30		6:30		6:30	
7:00		7:00		7:00		7:00	
7:30		7:30		7:30		7:30	
8:00		8:00		8:00		8:00	
8:30		8:30		8:30		8:30	
9:00		9:00		9:00		9:00	
9:30		9:30		9:30		9:30	
10:00		10:00		10:00		10:00	
10:30		10:30		10:30		10:30	
11:00		11:00		11:00		11:00	
11:30		11:30		11:30		11:30	
	I MEET MY GOALS		BUILDING MY DREAMS		NO EXCUSES		I AM AN AUTHOR
12:00		12:00		12:00		12:00	
12:30		12:30		12:30		12:30	
1:00		1:00		1:00		1:00	
1:30		1:30		1:30		1:30	
2:00		2:00		2:00		2:00	
2:30		2:30		2:30		2:30	
3:00		3:00		3:00		3:00	
3:30		3:30		3:30		3:30	
4:00		4:00		4:00		4:00	
4:30		4:30		4:30		4:30	
5:00		5:00		5:00		5:00	
5:30		5:30		5:30		5:30	
6:00		6:00		6:00		6:00	
6:30		6:30		6:30		6:30	
7:00		7:00		7:00		7:00	
7:30		7:30		7:30		7:30	
8:00		8:00		8:00		8:00	
WRITING PROGRESS		WRITING PROGRESS		WRITING PROGRESS		WRITING PROGRESS	

LOOKING AHEAD

Week Of

"You don't have to see the whole staircase. Just take the first step."
—Martin Luther King

PRIORITY GOALS

TO DO

DREAM GOALS

	MONDAY		TUESDAY		WEDNESDAY
	INTENTIONS		INTENTIONS		INTENTIONS
6:00		6:00		6:00	
6:30		6:30		6:30	
7:00		7:00		7:00	
7:30		7:30		7:30	
8:00		8:00		8:00	
8:30		8:30		8:30	
9:00		9:00		9:00	
9:30		9:30		9:30	
10:00		10:00		10:00	
10:30		10:30		10:30	
11:00		11:00		11:00	
11:30		11:30		11:30	
	I AM CREATIVE		MY WORDS MATTER		LIFE IS GOOD
12:00		12:00		12:00	
12:30		12:30		12:30	
1:00		1:00		1:00	
1:30		1:30		1:30	
2:00		2:00		2:00	
2:30		2:30		2:30	
3:00		3:00		3:00	
3:30		3:30		3:30	
4:00		4:00		4:00	
4:30		4:30		4:30	
5:00		5:00		5:00	
5:30		5:30		5:30	
6:00		6:00		6:00	
6:30		6:30		6:30	
7:00		7:00		7:00	
7:30		7:30		7:30	
8:00		8:00		8:00	
WRITING PROGRESS		WRITING PROGRESS		WRITING PROGRESS	
GRATITUDES					

THURSDAY		FRIDAY		SATURDAY		SUNDAY	
INTENTIONS		INTENTIONS		INTENTIONS		INTENTIONS	
6:00		6:00		6:00		6:00	
6:30		6:30		6:30		6:30	
7:00		7:00		7:00		7:00	
7:30		7:30		7:30		7:30	
8:00		8:00		8:00		8:00	
8:30		8:30		8:30		8:30	
9:00		9:00		9:00		9:00	
9:30		9:30		9:30		9:30	
10:00		10:00		10:00		10:00	
10:30		10:30		10:30		10:30	
11:00		11:00		11:00		11:00	
11:30		11:30		11:30		11:30	
	I MEET MY GOALS		BUILDING MY DREAMS		NO EXCUSES		I AM AN AUTHOR
12:00		12:00		12:00		12:00	
12:30		12:30		12:30		12:30	
1:00		1:00		1:00		1:00	
1:30		1:30		1:30		1:30	
2:00		2:00		2:00		2:00	
2:30		2:30		2:30		2:30	
3:00		3:00		3:00		3:00	
3:30		3:30		3:30		3:30	
4:00		4:00		4:00		4:00	
4:30		4:30		4:30		4:30	
5:00		5:00		5:00		5:00	
5:30		5:30		5:30		5:30	
6:00		6:00		6:00		6:00	
6:30		6:30		6:30		6:30	
7:00		7:00		7:00		7:00	
7:30		7:30		7:30		7:30	
8:00		8:00		8:00		8:00	
WRITING PROGRESS		WRITING PROGRESS		WRITING PROGRESS		WRITING PROGRESS	

LOOKING AHEAD

Week Of

"If you're waiting for permission… GRANTED!"
—*Demi Stevens*

PRIORITY GOALS

TO DO

DREAM GOALS

	MONDAY	TUESDAY	WEDNESDAY
	INTENTIONS	INTENTIONS	INTENTIONS
6:00			
6:30			
7:00			
7:30			
8:00			
8:30			
9:00			
9:30			
10:00			
10:30			
11:00			
11:30			
	I AM CREATIVE	MY WORDS MATTER	LIFE IS GOOD
12:00			
12:30			
1:00			
1:30			
2:00			
2:30			
3:00			
3:30			
4:00			
4:30			
5:00			
5:30			
6:00			
6:30			
7:00			
7:30			
8:00			
WRITING PROGRESS		WRITING PROGRESS	WRITING PROGRESS

GRATITUDES

THURSDAY		FRIDAY		SATURDAY		SUNDAY	
INTENTIONS		INTENTIONS		INTENTIONS		INTENTIONS	
6:00		6:00		6:00		6:00	
6:30		6:30		6:30		6:30	
7:00		7:00		7:00		7:00	
7:30		7:30		7:30		7:30	
8:00		8:00		8:00		8:00	
8:30		8:30		8:30		8:30	
9:00		9:00		9:00		9:00	
9:30		9:30		9:30		9:30	
10:00		10:00		10:00		10:00	
10:30		10:30		10:30		10:30	
11:00		11:00		11:00		11:00	
11:30		11:30		11:30		11:30	
	I MEET MY GOALS		BUILDING MY DREAMS		NO EXCUSES		I AM AN AUTHOR
12:00		12:00		12:00		12:00	
12:30		12:30		12:30		12:30	
1:00		1:00		1:00		1:00	
1:30		1:30		1:30		1:30	
2:00		2:00		2:00		2:00	
2:30		2:30		2:30		2:30	
3:00		3:00		3:00		3:00	
3:30		3:30		3:30		3:30	
4:00		4:00		4:00		4:00	
4:30		4:30		4:30		4:30	
5:00		5:00		5:00		5:00	
5:30		5:30		5:30		5:30	
6:00		6:00		6:00		6:00	
6:30		6:30		6:30		6:30	
7:00		7:00		7:00		7:00	
7:30		7:30		7:30		7:30	
8:00		8:00		8:00		8:00	
WRITING PROGRESS		WRITING PROGRESS		WRITING PROGRESS		WRITING PROGRESS	

LOOKING AHEAD

Monthly Overview

How did my writing go this month?

Did I meet my writing and personal goals? Why or why not?

Am I happy with how I spent my time?
If not, what changes will I make?

What did I learn this month that proved helpful?

What was my biggest time/ energy waster this month? How can I eliminate it?

What have I been procrastinating on?

FIND A PLACE TO SCHEDULE IT NEXT MONTH

What goals do I want to meet next month?

Month:

This Month's Focus

MONDAY	TUESDAY	WEDNESDAY

Social Media Goals

THURSDAY	FRIDAY	SATURDAY	SUNDAY

Sales / Releases / Queries

Week Of

"You can fix anything but a blank page."
—Nora Roberts

PRIORITY GOALS

TO DO

DREAM GOALS

	MONDAY		TUESDAY		WEDNESDAY	
	INTENTIONS		INTENTIONS		INTENTIONS	
6:00		6:00		6:00	
6:30		6:30		6:30	
7:00		7:00		7:00	
7:30		7:30		7:30	
8:00		8:00		8:00	
8:30		8:30		8:30	
9:00		9:00		9:00	
9:30		9:30		9:30	
10:00		10:00		10:00	
10:30		10:30		10:30	
11:00		11:00		11:00	
11:30		11:30		11:30	
	I AM CREATIVE		MY WORDS MATTER		LIFE IS GOOD	
12:00		12:00		12:00	
12:30		12:30		12:30	
1:00		1:00		1:00	
1:30		1:30		1:30	
2:00		2:00		2:00	
2:30		2:30		2:30	
3:00		3:00		3:00	
3:30		3:30		3:30	
4:00		4:00		4:00	
4:30		4:30		4:30	
5:00		5:00		5:00	
5:30		5:30		5:30	
6:00		6:00		6:00	
6:30		6:30		6:30	
7:00		7:00		7:00	
7:30		7:30		7:30	
8:00		8:00		8:00	
WRITING PROGRESS		WRITING PROGRESS		WRITING PROGRESS	
GRATITUDES					

THURSDAY		FRIDAY		SATURDAY		SUNDAY	
INTENTIONS		INTENTIONS		INTENTIONS		INTENTIONS	
6:00		6:00		6:00		6:00	
6:30		6:30		6:30		6:30	
7:00		7:00		7:00		7:00	
7:30		7:30		7:30		7:30	
8:00		8:00		8:00		8:00	
8:30		8:30		8:30		8:30	
9:00		9:00		9:00		9:00	
9:30		9:30		9:30		9:30	
10:00		10:00		10:00		10:00	
10:30		10:30		10:30		10:30	
11:00		11:00		11:00		11:00	
11:30		11:30		11:30		11:30	
	I MEET MY GOALS		BUILDING MY DREAMS		NO EXCUSES		I AM AN AUTHOR
12:00		12:00		12:00		12:00	
12:30		12:30		12:30		12:30	
1:00		1:00		1:00		1:00	
1:30		1:30		1:30		1:30	
2:00		2:00		2:00		2:00	
2:30		2:30		2:30		2:30	
3:00		3:00		3:00		3:00	
3:30		3:30		3:30		3:30	
4:00		4:00		4:00		4:00	
4:30		4:30		4:30		4:30	
5:00		5:00		5:00		5:00	
5:30		5:30		5:30		5:30	
6:00		6:00		6:00		6:00	
6:30		6:30		6:30		6:30	
7:00		7:00		7:00		7:00	
7:30		7:30		7:30		7:30	
8:00		8:00		8:00		8:00	
WRITING PROGRESS		WRITING PROGRESS		WRITING PROGRESS		WRITING PROGRESS	

LOOKING AHEAD

Week Of

"Start writing, no matter what. The water does not flow until the faucet is turned on."
—Louis L'Amour

PRIORITY GOALS

TO DO

DREAM GOALS

	MONDAY		TUESDAY		WEDNESDAY
	INTENTIONS		INTENTIONS		INTENTIONS
6:00		6:00		6:00	
6:30		6:30		6:30	
7:00		7:00		7:00	
7:30		7:30		7:30	
8:00		8:00		8:00	
8:30		8:30		8:30	
9:00		9:00		9:00	
9:30		9:30		9:30	
10:00		10:00		10:00	
10:30		10:30		10:30	
11:00		11:00		11:00	
11:30		11:30		11:30	
	I AM CREATIVE		MY WORDS MATTER		LIFE IS GOOD
12:00		12:00		12:00	
12:30		12:30		12:30	
1:00		1:00		1:00	
1:30		1:30		1:30	
2:00		2:00		2:00	
2:30		2:30		2:30	
3:00		3:00		3:00	
3:30		3:30		3:30	
4:00		4:00		4:00	
4:30		4:30		4:30	
5:00		5:00		5:00	
5:30		5:30		5:30	
6:00		6:00		6:00	
6:30		6:30		6:30	
7:00		7:00		7:00	
7:30		7:30		7:30	
8:00		8:00		8:00	
WRITING PROGRESS		WRITING PROGRESS		WRITING PROGRESS	

GRATITUDES

THURSDAY		FRIDAY		SATURDAY		SUNDAY	
INTENTIONS		INTENTIONS		INTENTIONS		INTENTIONS	
6:00		6:00		6:00		6:00	
6:30		6:30		6:30		6:30	
7:00		7:00		7:00		7:00	
7:30		7:30		7:30		7:30	
8:00		8:00		8:00		8:00	
8:30		8:30		8:30		8:30	
9:00		9:00		9:00		9:00	
9:30		9:30		9:30		9:30	
10:00		10:00		10:00		10:00	
10:30		10:30		10:30		10:30	
11:00		11:00		11:00		11:00	
11:30		11:30		11:30		11:30	
	I MEET MY GOALS		BUILDING MY DREAMS		NO EXCUSES		I AM AN AUTHOR
12:00		12:00		12:00		12:00	
12:30		12:30		12:30		12:30	
1:00		1:00		1:00		1:00	
1:30		1:30		1:30		1:30	
2:00		2:00		2:00		2:00	
2:30		2:30		2:30		2:30	
3:00		3:00		3:00		3:00	
3:30		3:30		3:30		3:30	
4:00		4:00		4:00		4:00	
4:30		4:30		4:30		4:30	
5:00		5:00		5:00		5:00	
5:30		5:30		5:30		5:30	
6:00		6:00		6:00		6:00	
6:30		6:30		6:30		6:30	
7:00		7:00		7:00		7:00	
7:30		7:30		7:30		7:30	
8:00		8:00		8:00		8:00	
WRITING PROGRESS		WRITING PROGRESS		WRITING PROGRESS		WRITING PROGRESS	

LOOKING AHEAD

Week Of

"A professional writer is an amateur who didn't quit."
—Richard Bach

PRIORITY GOALS

TO DO

DREAM GOALS

	MONDAY		TUESDAY		WEDNESDAY
	INTENTIONS		INTENTIONS		INTENTIONS
6:00		6:00		6:00	
6:30		6:30		6:30	
7:00		7:00		7:00	
7:30		7:30		7:30	
8:00		8:00		8:00	
8:30		8:30		8:30	
9:00		9:00		9:00	
9:30		9:30		9:30	
10:00		10:00		10:00	
10:30		10:30		10:30	
11:00		11:00		11:00	
11:30		11:30		11:30	
	I AM CREATIVE		MY WORDS MATTER		LIFE IS GOOD
12:00		12:00		12:00	
12:30		12:30		12:30	
1:00		1:00		1:00	
1:30		1:30		1:30	
2:00		2:00		2:00	
2:30		2:30		2:30	
3:00		3:00		3:00	
3:30		3:30		3:30	
4:00		4:00		4:00	
4:30		4:30		4:30	
5:00		5:00		5:00	
5:30		5:30		5:30	
6:00		6:00		6:00	
6:30		6:30		6:30	
7:00		7:00		7:00	
7:30		7:30		7:30	
8:00		8:00		8:00	
WRITING PROGRESS		WRITING PROGRESS		WRITING PROGRESS	

GRATITUDES

THURSDAY		FRIDAY		SATURDAY		SUNDAY	
INTENTIONS		INTENTIONS		INTENTIONS		INTENTIONS	
6:00		6:00		6:00		6:00	
6:30		6:30		6:30		6:30	
7:00		7:00		7:00		7:00	
7:30		7:30		7:30		7:30	
8:00		8:00		8:00		8:00	
8:30		8:30		8:30		8:30	
9:00		9:00		9:00		9:00	
9:30		9:30		9:30		9:30	
10:00		10:00		10:00		10:00	
10:30		10:30		10:30		10:30	
11:00		11:00		11:00		11:00	
11:30		11:30		11:30		11:30	
	I MEET MY GOALS		BUILDING MY DREAMS		NO EXCUSES		I AM AN AUTHOR
12:00		12:00		12:00		12:00	
12:30		12:30		12:30		12:30	
1:00		1:00		1:00		1:00	
1:30		1:30		1:30		1:30	
2:00		2:00		2:00		2:00	
2:30		2:30		2:30		2:30	
3:00		3:00		3:00		3:00	
3:30		3:30		3:30		3:30	
4:00		4:00		4:00		4:00	
4:30		4:30		4:30		4:30	
5:00		5:00		5:00		5:00	
5:30		5:30		5:30		5:30	
6:00		6:00		6:00		6:00	
6:30		6:30		6:30		6:30	
7:00		7:00		7:00		7:00	
7:30		7:30		7:30		7:30	
8:00		8:00		8:00		8:00	
WRITING PROGRESS		WRITING PROGRESS		WRITING PROGRESS		WRITING PROGRESS	

LOOKING AHEAD

Week Of

"When you say 'yes' to others, make sure you are not saying 'no' to yourself."
—Pablo Coehlo

PRIORITY GOALS

TO DO

DREAM GOALS

	MONDAY		TUESDAY		WEDNESDAY
	INTENTIONS		INTENTIONS		INTENTIONS
6:00		6:00		6:00	
6:30		6:30		6:30	
7:00		7:00		7:00	
7:30		7:30		7:30	
8:00		8:00		8:00	
8:30		8:30		8:30	
9:00		9:00		9:00	
9:30		9:30		9:30	
10:00		10:00		10:00	
10:30		10:30		10:30	
11:00		11:00		11:00	
11:30		11:30		11:30	
	I AM CREATIVE		MY WORDS MATTER		LIFE IS GOOD
12:00		12:00		12:00	
12:30		12:30		12:30	
1:00		1:00		1:00	
1:30		1:30		1:30	
2:00		2:00		2:00	
2:30		2:30		2:30	
3:00		3:00		3:00	
3:30		3:30		3:30	
4:00		4:00		4:00	
4:30		4:30		4:30	
5:00		5:00		5:00	
5:30		5:30		5:30	
6:00		6:00		6:00	
6:30		6:30		6:30	
7:00		7:00		7:00	
7:30		7:30		7:30	
8:00		8:00		8:00	
WRITING PROGRESS		WRITING PROGRESS		WRITING PROGRESS	
GRATITUDES					

THURSDAY		FRIDAY		SATURDAY		SUNDAY	
INTENTIONS		**INTENTIONS**		**INTENTIONS**		**INTENTIONS**	
6:00		6:00		6:00		6:00	
6:30		6:30		6:30		6:30	
7:00		7:00		7:00		7:00	
7:30		7:30		7:30		7:30	
8:00		8:00		8:00		8:00	
8:30		8:30		8:30		8:30	
9:00		9:00		9:00		9:00	
9:30		9:30		9:30		9:30	
10:00		10:00		10:00		10:00	
10:30		10:30		10:30		10:30	
11:00		11:00		11:00		11:00	
11:30		11:30		11:30		11:30	
	I MEET MY GOALS		BUILDING MY DREAMS		NO EXCUSES		I AM AN AUTHOR
12:00		12:00		12:00		12:00	
12:30		12:30		12:30		12:30	
1:00		1:00		1:00		1:00	
1:30		1:30		1:30		1:30	
2:00		2:00		2:00		2:00	
2:30		2:30		2:30		2:30	
3:00		3:00		3:00		3:00	
3:30		3:30		3:30		3:30	
4:00		4:00		4:00		4:00	
4:30		4:30		4:30		4:30	
5:00		5:00		5:00		5:00	
5:30		5:30		5:30		5:30	
6:00		6:00		6:00		6:00	
6:30		6:30		6:30		6:30	
7:00		7:00		7:00		7:00	
7:30		7:30		7:30		7:30	
8:00		8:00		8:00		8:00	
WRITING PROGRESS		**WRITING PROGRESS**		**WRITING PROGRESS**		**WRITING PROGRESS**	

LOOKING AHEAD

Monthly Overview

How did my writing go this month?

Did I meet my writing and personal goals? Why or why not?

Am I happy with how I spent my time?
If not, what changes will I make?

What did I learn this month that proved helpful?

What was my biggest time/ energy waster this month? How can I eliminate it?

What have I been procrastinating on?

FIND A PLACE TO SCHEDULE IT NEXT MONTH

What goals do I want to meet next month?

Month:

This Month's Focus

MONDAY	TUESDAY	WEDNESDAY

Social Media Goals

THURSDAY	FRIDAY	SATURDAY	SUNDAY

 Sales / Releases / Queries

Week Of

"Write the life of your dreams. Then find a way to live it!"
—Demi Stevens

PRIORITY GOALS

TO DO

DREAM GOALS

	MONDAY	TUESDAY	WEDNESDAY
	INTENTIONS	INTENTIONS	INTENTIONS
6:00			
6:30			
7:00			
7:30			
8:00			
8:30			
9:00			
9:30			
10:00			
10:30			
11:00			
11:30			
	I AM CREATIVE	MY WORDS MATTER	LIFE IS GOOD
12:00			
12:30			
1:00			
1:30			
2:00			
2:30			
3:00			
3:30			
4:00			
4:30			
5:00			
5:30			
6:00			
6:30			
7:00			
7:30			
8:00			
	WRITING PROGRESS	WRITING PROGRESS	WRITING PROGRESS

GRATITUDES

THURSDAY		FRIDAY		SATURDAY		SUNDAY	
INTENTIONS		INTENTIONS		INTENTIONS		INTENTIONS	
6:00		6:00		6:00		6:00	
6:30		6:30		6:30		6:30	
7:00		7:00		7:00		7:00	
7:30		7:30		7:30		7:30	
8:00		8:00		8:00		8:00	
8:30		8:30		8:30		8:30	
9:00		9:00		9:00		9:00	
9:30		9:30		9:30		9:30	
10:00		10:00		10:00		10:00	
10:30		10:30		10:30		10:30	
11:00		11:00		11:00		11:00	
11:30		11:30		11:30		11:30	
	I MEET MY GOALS		BUILDING MY DREAMS		NO EXCUSES		I AM AN AUTHOR
12:00		12:00		12:00		12:00	
12:30		12:30		12:30		12:30	
1:00		1:00		1:00		1:00	
1:30		1:30		1:30		1:30	
2:00		2:00		2:00		2:00	
2:30		2:30		2:30		2:30	
3:00		3:00		3:00		3:00	
3:30		3:30		3:30		3:30	
4:00		4:00		4:00		4:00	
4:30		4:30		4:30		4:30	
5:00		5:00		5:00		5:00	
5:30		5:30		5:30		5:30	
6:00		6:00		6:00		6:00	
6:30		6:30		6:30		6:30	
7:00		7:00		7:00		7:00	
7:30		7:30		7:30		7:30	
8:00		8:00		8:00		8:00	
WRITING PROGRESS		WRITING PROGRESS		WRITING PROGRESS		WRITING PROGRESS	

LOOKING AHEAD

Week Of

"Always be a first-rate version of yourself, instead of a second-rate version of somebody else."
—Judy Garland

PRIORITY GOALS

TO DO

DREAM GOALS

	MONDAY		TUESDAY		WEDNESDAY
	INTENTIONS		INTENTIONS		INTENTIONS
6:00		6:00		6:00	
6:30		6:30		6:30	
7:00		7:00		7:00	
7:30		7:30		7:30	
8:00		8:00		8:00	
8:30		8:30		8:30	
9:00		9:00		9:00	
9:30		9:30		9:30	
10:00		10:00		10:00	
10:30		10:30		10:30	
11:00		11:00		11:00	
11:30		11:30		11:30	
	I AM CREATIVE		MY WORDS MATTER		LIFE IS GOOD
12:00		12:00		12:00	
12:30		12:30		12:30	
1:00		1:00		1:00	
1:30		1:30		1:30	
2:00		2:00		2:00	
2:30		2:30		2:30	
3:00		3:00		3:00	
3:30		3:30		3:30	
4:00		4:00		4:00	
4:30		4:30		4:30	
5:00		5:00		5:00	
5:30		5:30		5:30	
6:00		6:00		6:00	
6:30		6:30		6:30	
7:00		7:00		7:00	
7:30		7:30		7:30	
8:00		8:00		8:00	
WRITING PROGRESS		WRITING PROGRESS		WRITING PROGRESS	
GRATITUDES					

THURSDAY		FRIDAY		SATURDAY		SUNDAY	
INTENTIONS		INTENTIONS		INTENTIONS		INTENTIONS	
6:00		6:00		6:00		6:00	
6:30		6:30		6:30		6:30	
7:00		7:00		7:00		7:00	
7:30		7:30		7:30		7:30	
8:00		8:00		8:00		8:00	
8:30		8:30		8:30		8:30	
9:00		9:00		9:00		9:00	
9:30		9:30		9:30		9:30	
10:00		10:00		10:00		10:00	
10:30		10:30		10:30		10:30	
11:00		11:00		11:00		11:00	
11:30		11:30		11:30		11:30	
	I MEET MY GOALS		BUILDING MY DREAMS		NO EXCUSES		I AM AN AUTHOR
12:00		12:00		12:00		12:00	
12:30		12:30		12:30		12:30	
1:00		1:00		1:00		1:00	
1:30		1:30		1:30		1:30	
2:00		2:00		2:00		2:00	
2:30		2:30		2:30		2:30	
3:00		3:00		3:00		3:00	
3:30		3:30		3:30		3:30	
4:00		4:00		4:00		4:00	
4:30		4:30		4:30		4:30	
5:00		5:00		5:00		5:00	
5:30		5:30		5:30		5:30	
6:00		6:00		6:00		6:00	
6:30		6:30		6:30		6:30	
7:00		7:00		7:00		7:00	
7:30		7:30		7:30		7:30	
8:00		8:00		8:00		8:00	
WRITING PROGRESS		WRITING PROGRESS		WRITING PROGRESS		WRITING PROGRESS	

LOOKING AHEAD

Week Of

"Writing is the only thing that, when I do it, I don't feel I should be doing something else."
—Gloria Steinem

PRIORITY GOALS

TO DO

DREAM GOALS

	MONDAY	TUESDAY	WEDNESDAY
	INTENTIONS	**INTENTIONS**	**INTENTIONS**
6:00		6:00		6:00	
6:30		6:30		6:30	
7:00		7:00		7:00	
7:30		7:30		7:30	
8:00		8:00		8:00	
8:30		8:30		8:30	
9:00		9:00		9:00	
9:30		9:30		9:30	
10:00		10:00		10:00	
10:30		10:30		10:30	
11:00		11:00		11:00	
11:30		11:30		11:30	
	I AM CREATIVE		**MY WORDS MATTER**		**LIFE IS GOOD**
12:00		12:00		12:00	
12:30		12:30		12:30	
1:00		1:00		1:00	
1:30		1:30		1:30	
2:00		2:00		2:00	
2:30		2:30		2:30	
3:00		3:00		3:00	
3:30		3:30		3:30	
4:00		4:00		4:00	
4:30		4:30		4:30	
5:00		5:00		5:00	
5:30		5:30		5:30	
6:00		6:00		6:00	
6:30		6:30		6:30	
7:00		7:00		7:00	
7:30		7:30		7:30	
8:00		8:00		8:00	
WRITING PROGRESS		**WRITING PROGRESS**		**WRITING PROGRESS**	

GRATITUDES

THURSDAY		FRIDAY		SATURDAY		SUNDAY	
INTENTIONS		INTENTIONS		INTENTIONS		INTENTIONS	
6:00		6:00		6:00		6:00	
6:30		6:30		6:30		6:30	
7:00		7:00		7:00		7:00	
7:30		7:30		7:30		7:30	
8:00		8:00		8:00		8:00	
8:30		8:30		8:30		8:30	
9:00		9:00		9:00		9:00	
9:30		9:30		9:30		9:30	
10:00		10:00		10:00		10:00	
10:30		10:30		10:30		10:30	
11:00		11:00		11:00		11:00	
11:30		11:30		11:30		11:30	
	I MEET MY GOALS		BUILDING MY DREAMS		NO EXCUSES		I AM AN AUTHOR
12:00		12:00		12:00		12:00	
12:30		12:30		12:30		12:30	
1:00		1:00		1:00		1:00	
1:30		1:30		1:30		1:30	
2:00		2:00		2:00		2:00	
2:30		2:30		2:30		2:30	
3:00		3:00		3:00		3:00	
3:30		3:30		3:30		3:30	
4:00		4:00		4:00		4:00	
4:30		4:30		4:30		4:30	
5:00		5:00		5:00		5:00	
5:30		5:30		5:30		5:30	
6:00		6:00		6:00		6:00	
6:30		6:30		6:30		6:30	
7:00		7:00		7:00		7:00	
7:30		7:30		7:30		7:30	
8:00		8:00		8:00		8:00	
WRITING PROGRESS		WRITING PROGRESS		WRITING PROGRESS		WRITING PROGRESS	

LOOKING AHEAD

Week Of

"If my words reach just one person... I'm glad they reached you!"
—Demi Stevens

PRIORITY GOALS

TO DO

DREAM GOALS

	MONDAY	TUESDAY	WEDNESDAY
	INTENTIONS	INTENTIONS	INTENTIONS
6:00			
6:30			
7:00			
7:30			
8:00			
8:30			
9:00			
9:30			
10:00			
10:30			
11:00			
11:30			
	I AM CREATIVE	MY WORDS MATTER	LIFE IS GOOD
12:00			
12:30			
1:00			
1:30			
2:00			
2:30			
3:00			
3:30			
4:00			
4:30			
5:00			
5:30			
6:00			
6:30			
7:00			
7:30			
8:00			
WRITING PROGRESS		WRITING PROGRESS	WRITING PROGRESS
GRATITUDES			

THURSDAY		FRIDAY		SATURDAY		SUNDAY	
INTENTIONS		INTENTIONS		INTENTIONS		INTENTIONS	
6:00		6:00		6:00		6:00	
6:30		6:30		6:30		6:30	
7:00		7:00		7:00		7:00	
7:30		7:30		7:30		7:30	
8:00		8:00		8:00		8:00	
8:30		8:30		8:30		8:30	
9:00		9:00		9:00		9:00	
9:30		9:30		9:30		9:30	
10:00		10:00		10:00		10:00	
10:30		10:30		10:30		10:30	
11:00		11:00		11:00		11:00	
11:30		11:30		11:30		11:30	
	I MEET MY GOALS		BUILDING MY DREAMS		NO EXCUSES		I AM AN AUTHOR
12:00		12:00		12:00		12:00	
12:30		12:30		12:30		12:30	
1:00		1:00		1:00		1:00	
1:30		1:30		1:30		1:30	
2:00		2:00		2:00		2:00	
2:30		2:30		2:30		2:30	
3:00		3:00		3:00		3:00	
3:30		3:30		3:30		3:30	
4:00		4:00		4:00		4:00	
4:30		4:30		4:30		4:30	
5:00		5:00		5:00		5:00	
5:30		5:30		5:30		5:30	
6:00		6:00		6:00		6:00	
6:30		6:30		6:30		6:30	
7:00		7:00		7:00		7:00	
7:30		7:30		7:30		7:30	
8:00		8:00		8:00		8:00	
WRITING PROGRESS		WRITING PROGRESS		WRITING PROGRESS		WRITING PROGRESS	

LOOKING AHEAD

Quarterly Overview

**Am I still on target with my yearly goals?
Or have I chosen a new path?**

What interfered with my progress?

What can I do next quarter to eliminate these obstacles?

What do I need to let go of this coming quarter?

What happened this quarter that I need to reframe positively?

How do my work and activities reflect the yearly word I chose?

What do I hope to accomplish next quarter?

Month:

This Month's Focus

MONDAY	TUESDAY	WEDNESDAY

Social Media Goals

THURSDAY	FRIDAY	SATURDAY	SUNDAY

 Sales / Releases / Queries

Week Of

"You are the average of the five people you spend the most time with."
—*Jim Rohn*

PRIORITY GOALS

TO DO

DREAM GOALS

	MONDAY		TUESDAY		WEDNESDAY
	INTENTIONS		**INTENTIONS**		**INTENTIONS**
6:00		6:00		6:00	
6:30		6:30		6:30	
7:00		7:00		7:00	
7:30		7:30		7:30	
8:00		8:00		8:00	
8:30		8:30		8:30	
9:00		9:00		9:00	
9:30		9:30		9:30	
10:00		10:00		10:00	
10:30		10:30		10:30	
11:00		11:00		11:00	
11:30		11:30		11:30	
	I AM CREATIVE		**MY WORDS MATTER**		**LIFE IS GOOD**
12:00		12:00		12:00	
12:30		12:30		12:30	
1:00		1:00		1:00	
1:30		1:30		1:30	
2:00		2:00		2:00	
2:30		2:30		2:30	
3:00		3:00		3:00	
3:30		3:30		3:30	
4:00		4:00		4:00	
4:30		4:30		4:30	
5:00		5:00		5:00	
5:30		5:30		5:30	
6:00		6:00		6:00	
6:30		6:30		6:30	
7:00		7:00		7:00	
7:30		7:30		7:30	
8:00		8:00		8:00	
WRITING PROGRESS		**WRITING PROGRESS**		**WRITING PROGRESS**	

GRATITUDES

THURSDAY		FRIDAY		SATURDAY		SUNDAY	
INTENTIONS		INTENTIONS		INTENTIONS		INTENTIONS	
6:00		6:00		6:00		6:00	
6:30		6:30		6:30		6:30	
7:00		7:00		7:00		7:00	
7:30		7:30		7:30		7:30	
8:00		8:00		8:00		8:00	
8:30		8:30		8:30		8:30	
9:00		9:00		9:00		9:00	
9:30		9:30		9:30		9:30	
10:00		10:00		10:00		10:00	
10:30		10:30		10:30		10:30	
11:00		11:00		11:00		11:00	
11:30		11:30		11:30		11:30	
	I MEET MY GOALS		BUILDING MY DREAMS		NO EXCUSES		I AM AN AUTHOR
12:00		12:00		12:00		12:00	
12:30		12:30		12:30		12:30	
1:00		1:00		1:00		1:00	
1:30		1:30		1:30		1:30	
2:00		2:00		2:00		2:00	
2:30		2:30		2:30		2:30	
3:00		3:00		3:00		3:00	
3:30		3:30		3:30		3:30	
4:00		4:00		4:00		4:00	
4:30		4:30		4:30		4:30	
5:00		5:00		5:00		5:00	
5:30		5:30		5:30		5:30	
6:00		6:00		6:00		6:00	
6:30		6:30		6:30		6:30	
7:00		7:00		7:00		7:00	
7:30		7:30		7:30		7:30	
8:00		8:00		8:00		8:00	
WRITING PROGRESS		WRITING PROGRESS		WRITING PROGRESS		WRITING PROGRESS	

LOOKING AHEAD

Week Of

"It doesn't matter how many book ideas you have if you can't finish writing your book."
—Joe Bunting

PRIORITY GOALS

TO DO

DREAM GOALS

	MONDAY		TUESDAY		WEDNESDAY
	INTENTIONS		INTENTIONS		INTENTIONS
6:00		6:00		6:00	
6:30		6:30		6:30	
7:00		7:00		7:00	
7:30		7:30		7:30	
8:00		8:00		8:00	
8:30		8:30		8:30	
9:00		9:00		9:00	
9:30		9:30		9:30	
10:00		10:00		10:00	
10:30		10:30		10:30	
11:00		11:00		11:00	
11:30		11:30		11:30	
	I AM CREATIVE		MY WORDS MATTER		LIFE IS GOOD
12:00		12:00		12:00	
12:30		12:30		12:30	
1:00		1:00		1:00	
1:30		1:30		1:30	
2:00		2:00		2:00	
2:30		2:30		2:30	
3:00		3:00		3:00	
3:30		3:30		3:30	
4:00		4:00		4:00	
4:30		4:30		4:30	
5:00		5:00		5:00	
5:30		5:30		5:30	
6:00		6:00		6:00	
6:30		6:30		6:30	
7:00		7:00		7:00	
7:30		7:30		7:30	
8:00		8:00		8:00	
WRITING PROGRESS		WRITING PROGRESS		WRITING PROGRESS	

GRATITUDES

THURSDAY		FRIDAY		SATURDAY		SUNDAY	
INTENTIONS		INTENTIONS		INTENTIONS		INTENTIONS	
6:00		6:00		6:00		6:00	
6:30		6:30		6:30		6:30	
7:00		7:00		7:00		7:00	
7:30		7:30		7:30		7:30	
8:00		8:00		8:00		8:00	
8:30		8:30		8:30		8:30	
9:00		9:00		9:00		9:00	
9:30		9:30		9:30		9:30	
10:00		10:00		10:00		10:00	
10:30		10:30		10:30		10:30	
11:00		11:00		11:00		11:00	
11:30		11:30		11:30		11:30	
	I MEET MY GOALS		BUILDING MY DREAMS		NO EXCUSES		I AM AN AUTHOR
12:00		12:00		12:00		12:00	
12:30		12:30		12:30		12:30	
1:00		1:00		1:00		1:00	
1:30		1:30		1:30		1:30	
2:00		2:00		2:00		2:00	
2:30		2:30		2:30		2:30	
3:00		3:00		3:00		3:00	
3:30		3:30		3:30		3:30	
4:00		4:00		4:00		4:00	
4:30		4:30		4:30		4:30	
5:00		5:00		5:00		5:00	
5:30		5:30		5:30		5:30	
6:00		6:00		6:00		6:00	
6:30		6:30		6:30		6:30	
7:00		7:00		7:00		7:00	
7:30		7:30		7:30		7:30	
8:00		8:00		8:00		8:00	
WRITING PROGRESS		WRITING PROGRESS		WRITING PROGRESS		WRITING PROGRESS	

LOOKING AHEAD

Week Of

"Make the most of yourself by fanning the tiny inner sparks of possibility into flames of achievement."
—Golda Meir

PRIORITY GOALS

TO DO

DREAM GOALS

	MONDAY		TUESDAY		WEDNESDAY
	INTENTIONS		INTENTIONS		INTENTIONS
6:00		6:00		6:00	
6:30		6:30		6:30	
7:00		7:00		7:00	
7:30		7:30		7:30	
8:00		8:00		8:00	
8:30		8:30		8:30	
9:00		9:00		9:00	
9:30		9:30		9:30	
10:00		10:00		10:00	
10:30		10:30		10:30	
11:00		11:00		11:00	
11:30		11:30		11:30	
	I AM CREATIVE		MY WORDS MATTER		LIFE IS GOOD
12:00		12:00		12:00	
12:30		12:30		12:30	
1:00		1:00		1:00	
1:30		1:30		1:30	
2:00		2:00		2:00	
2:30		2:30		2:30	
3:00		3:00		3:00	
3:30		3:30		3:30	
4:00		4:00		4:00	
4:30		4:30		4:30	
5:00		5:00		5:00	
5:30		5:30		5:30	
6:00		6:00		6:00	
6:30		6:30		6:30	
7:00		7:00		7:00	
7:30		7:30		7:30	
8:00		8:00		8:00	
WRITING PROGRESS		WRITING PROGRESS		WRITING PROGRESS	
GRATITUDES					

THURSDAY	FRIDAY	SATURDAY	SUNDAY
INTENTIONS	INTENTIONS	INTENTIONS	INTENTIONS
6:00	6:00	6:00	6:00
6:30	6:30	6:30	6:30
7:00	7:00	7:00	7:00
7:30	7:30	7:30	7:30
8:00	8:00	8:00	8:00
8:30	8:30	8:30	8:30
9:00	9:00	9:00	9:00
9:30	9:30	9:30	9:30
10:00	10:00	10:00	10:00
10:30	10:30	10:30	10:30
11:00	11:00	11:00	11:00
11:30	11:30	11:30	11:30
I MEET MY GOALS	BUILDING MY DREAMS	NO EXCUSES	I AM AN AUTHOR
12:00	12:00	12:00	12:00
12:30	12:30	12:30	12:30
1:00	1:00	1:00	1:00
1:30	1:30	1:30	1:30
2:00	2:00	2:00	2:00
2:30	2:30	2:30	2:30
3:00	3:00	3:00	3:00
3:30	3:30	3:30	3:30
4:00	4:00	4:00	4:00
4:30	4:30	4:30	4:30
5:00	5:00	5:00	5:00
5:30	5:30	5:30	5:30
6:00	6:00	6:00	6:00
6:30	6:30	6:30	6:30
7:00	7:00	7:00	7:00
7:30	7:30	7:30	7:30
8:00	8:00	8:00	8:00
WRITING PROGRESS	WRITING PROGRESS	WRITING PROGRESS	WRITING PROGRESS

LOOKING AHEAD

Week Of

"Very few writers really know what they are doing until they've done it."
—Anne Lamott

PRIORITY GOALS

TO DO

DREAM GOALS

	MONDAY		TUESDAY		WEDNESDAY
	INTENTIONS		INTENTIONS		INTENTIONS
6:00		6:00		6:00	
6:30		6:30		6:30	
7:00		7:00		7:00	
7:30		7:30		7:30	
8:00		8:00		8:00	
8:30		8:30		8:30	
9:00		9:00		9:00	
9:30		9:30		9:30	
10:00		10:00		10:00	
10:30		10:30		10:30	
11:00		11:00		11:00	
11:30		11:30		11:30	
	I AM CREATIVE		MY WORDS MATTER		LIFE IS GOOD
12:00		12:00		12:00	
12:30		12:30		12:30	
1:00		1:00		1:00	
1:30		1:30		1:30	
2:00		2:00		2:00	
2:30		2:30		2:30	
3:00		3:00		3:00	
3:30		3:30		3:30	
4:00		4:00		4:00	
4:30		4:30		4:30	
5:00		5:00		5:00	
5:30		5:30		5:30	
6:00		6:00		6:00	
6:30		6:30		6:30	
7:00		7:00		7:00	
7:30		7:30		7:30	
8:00		8:00		8:00	
WRITING PROGRESS		WRITING PROGRESS		WRITING PROGRESS	

GRATITUDES

THURSDAY		FRIDAY		SATURDAY		SUNDAY	
INTENTIONS		**INTENTIONS**		**INTENTIONS**		**INTENTIONS**	
6:00		6:00		6:00		6:00	
6:30		6:30		6:30		6:30	
7:00		7:00		7:00		7:00	
7:30		7:30		7:30		7:30	
8:00		8:00		8:00		8:00	
8:30		8:30		8:30		8:30	
9:00		9:00		9:00		9:00	
9:30		9:30		9:30		9:30	
10:00		10:00		10:00		10:00	
10:30		10:30		10:30		10:30	
11:00		11:00		11:00		11:00	
11:30		11:30		11:30		11:30	
	I MEET MY GOALS		BUILDING MY DREAMS		NO EXCUSES		I AM AN AUTHOR
12:00		12:00		12:00		12:00	
12:30		12:30		12:30		12:30	
1:00		1:00		1:00		1:00	
1:30		1:30		1:30		1:30	
2:00		2:00		2:00		2:00	
2:30		2:30		2:30		2:30	
3:00		3:00		3:00		3:00	
3:30		3:30		3:30		3:30	
4:00		4:00		4:00		4:00	
4:30		4:30		4:30		4:30	
5:00		5:00		5:00		5:00	
5:30		5:30		5:30		5:30	
6:00		6:00		6:00		6:00	
6:30		6:30		6:30		6:30	
7:00		7:00		7:00		7:00	
7:30		7:30		7:30		7:30	
8:00		8:00		8:00		8:00	
WRITING PROGRESS		**WRITING PROGRESS**		**WRITING PROGRESS**		**WRITING PROGRESS**	

LOOKING AHEAD

Week Of

"Cultivate the habit of being grateful for every good thing that comes to you…"
—Ralph Waldo Emerson

PRIORITY GOALS

TO DO

DREAM GOALS

	MONDAY		TUESDAY		WEDNESDAY	
	INTENTIONS		**INTENTIONS**		**INTENTIONS**	
	6:00		6:00		6:00	
	6:30		6:30		6:30	
	7:00		7:00		7:00	
	7:30		7:30		7:30	
	8:00		8:00		8:00	
	8:30		8:30		8:30	
	9:00		9:00		9:00	
	9:30		9:30		9:30	
	10:00		10:00		10:00	
	10:30		10:30		10:30	
	11:00		11:00		11:00	
	11:30		11:30		11:30	
	I AM CREATIVE		**MY WORDS MATTER**		**LIFE IS GOOD**	
	12:00		12:00		12:00	
	12:30		12:30		12:30	
	1:00		1:00		1:00	
	1:30		1:30		1:30	
	2:00		2:00		2:00	
	2:30		2:30		2:30	
	3:00		3:00		3:00	
	3:30		3:30		3:30	
	4:00		4:00		4:00	
	4:30		4:30		4:30	
	5:00		5:00		5:00	
	5:30		5:30		5:30	
	6:00		6:00		6:00	
	6:30		6:30		6:30	
	7:00		7:00		7:00	
	7:30		7:30		7:30	
	8:00		8:00		8:00	
	WRITING PROGRESS		**WRITING PROGRESS**		**WRITING PROGRESS**	

GRATITUDES

THURSDAY		FRIDAY		SATURDAY		SUNDAY	
INTENTIONS		INTENTIONS		INTENTIONS		INTENTIONS	
6:00		6:00		6:00		6:00	
6:30		6:30		6:30		6:30	
7:00		7:00		7:00		7:00	
7:30		7:30		7:30		7:30	
8:00		8:00		8:00		8:00	
8:30		8:30		8:30		8:30	
9:00		9:00		9:00		9:00	
9:30		9:30		9:30		9:30	
10:00		10:00		10:00		10:00	
10:30		10:30		10:30		10:30	
11:00		11:00		11:00		11:00	
11:30		11:30		11:30		11:30	
	I MEET MY GOALS		BUILDING MY DREAMS		NO EXCUSES		I AM AN AUTHOR
12:00		12:00		12:00		12:00	
12:30		12:30		12:30		12:30	
1:00		1:00		1:00		1:00	
1:30		1:30		1:30		1:30	
2:00		2:00		2:00		2:00	
2:30		2:30		2:30		2:30	
3:00		3:00		3:00		3:00	
3:30		3:30		3:30		3:30	
4:00		4:00		4:00		4:00	
4:30		4:30		4:30		4:30	
5:00		5:00		5:00		5:00	
5:30		5:30		5:30		5:30	
6:00		6:00		6:00		6:00	
6:30		6:30		6:30		6:30	
7:00		7:00		7:00		7:00	
7:30		7:30		7:30		7:30	
8:00		8:00		8:00		8:00	
WRITING PROGRESS		WRITING PROGRESS		WRITING PROGRESS		WRITING PROGRESS	

LOOKING AHEAD

Monthly Overview

How did my writing go this month?

Did I meet my writing and personal goals? Why or why not?

**Am I happy with how I spent my time?
If not, what changes will I make?**

What did I learn this month that proved helpful?

What was my biggest time/ energy waster this month? How can I eliminate it?

What have I been procrastinating on?

FIND A PLACE TO SCHEDULE IT NEXT MONTH

What goals do I want to meet next month?

Month:

MONDAY	TUESDAY	WEDNESDAY

This Month's Focus

Social Media Goals

THURSDAY	FRIDAY	SATURDAY	SUNDAY

 Sales / Releases / Queries

Week Of

"Less procrastinating, more WRITING!"
—Demi Stevens

PRIORITY GOALS

TO DO

DREAM GOALS

	MONDAY		TUESDAY		WEDNESDAY
	INTENTIONS		**INTENTIONS**		**INTENTIONS**
6:00		6:00		6:00	
6:30		6:30		6:30	
7:00		7:00		7:00	
7:30		7:30		7:30	
8:00		8:00		8:00	
8:30		8:30		8:30	
9:00		9:00		9:00	
9:30		9:30		9:30	
10:00		10:00		10:00	
10:30		10:30		10:30	
11:00		11:00		11:00	
11:30		11:30		11:30	
	I AM CREATIVE		**MY WORDS MATTER**		**LIFE IS GOOD**
12:00		12:00		12:00	
12:30		12:30		12:30	
1:00		1:00		1:00	
1:30		1:30		1:30	
2:00		2:00		2:00	
2:30		2:30		2:30	
3:00		3:00		3:00	
3:30		3:30		3:30	
4:00		4:00		4:00	
4:30		4:30		4:30	
5:00		5:00		5:00	
5:30		5:30		5:30	
6:00		6:00		6:00	
6:30		6:30		6:30	
7:00		7:00		7:00	
7:30		7:30		7:30	
8:00		8:00		8:00	
WRITING PROGRESS		**WRITING PROGRESS**		**WRITING PROGRESS**	
GRATITUDES					

THURSDAY		FRIDAY		SATURDAY		SUNDAY	
INTENTIONS		INTENTIONS		INTENTIONS		INTENTIONS	
6:00		6:00		6:00		6:00	
6:30		6:30		6:30		6:30	
7:00		7:00		7:00		7:00	
7:30		7:30		7:30		7:30	
8:00		8:00		8:00		8:00	
8:30		8:30		8:30		8:30	
9:00		9:00		9:00		9:00	
9:30		9:30		9:30		9:30	
10:00		10:00		10:00		10:00	
10:30		10:30		10:30		10:30	
11:00		11:00		11:00		11:00	
11:30		11:30		11:30		11:30	
	I MEET MY GOALS		BUILDING MY DREAMS		NO EXCUSES		I AM AN AUTHOR
12:00		12:00		12:00		12:00	
12:30		12:30		12:30		12:30	
1:00		1:00		1:00		1:00	
1:30		1:30		1:30		1:30	
2:00		2:00		2:00		2:00	
2:30		2:30		2:30		2:30	
3:00		3:00		3:00		3:00	
3:30		3:30		3:30		3:30	
4:00		4:00		4:00		4:00	
4:30		4:30		4:30		4:30	
5:00		5:00		5:00		5:00	
5:30		5:30		5:30		5:30	
6:00		6:00		6:00		6:00	
6:30		6:30		6:30		6:30	
7:00		7:00		7:00		7:00	
7:30		7:30		7:30		7:30	
8:00		8:00		8:00		8:00	
WRITING PROGRESS		WRITING PROGRESS		WRITING PROGRESS		WRITING PROGRESS	

LOOKING AHEAD

Week Of

"We cannot solve problems with the same thinking we used when we created them."
—Albert Einstein

PRIORITY GOALS

TO DO

DREAM GOALS

	MONDAY		TUESDAY		WEDNESDAY
	INTENTIONS		INTENTIONS		INTENTIONS
6:00		6:00		6:00	
6:30		6:30		6:30	
7:00		7:00		7:00	
7:30		7:30		7:30	
8:00		8:00		8:00	
8:30		8:30		8:30	
9:00		9:00		9:00	
9:30		9:30		9:30	
10:00		10:00		10:00	
10:30		10:30		10:30	
11:00		11:00		11:00	
11:30		11:30		11:30	
	I AM CREATIVE		MY WORDS MATTER		LIFE IS GOOD
12:00		12:00		12:00	
12:30		12:30		12:30	
1:00		1:00		1:00	
1:30		1:30		1:30	
2:00		2:00		2:00	
2:30		2:30		2:30	
3:00		3:00		3:00	
3:30		3:30		3:30	
4:00		4:00		4:00	
4:30		4:30		4:30	
5:00		5:00		5:00	
5:30		5:30		5:30	
6:00		6:00		6:00	
6:30		6:30		6:30	
7:00		7:00		7:00	
7:30		7:30		7:30	
8:00		8:00		8:00	
WRITING PROGRESS		WRITING PROGRESS		WRITING PROGRESS	

GRATITUDES

THURSDAY		FRIDAY		SATURDAY		SUNDAY	
INTENTIONS		INTENTIONS		INTENTIONS		INTENTIONS	
6:00		6:00		6:00		6:00	
6:30		6:30		6:30		6:30	
7:00		7:00		7:00		7:00	
7:30		7:30		7:30		7:30	
8:00		8:00		8:00		8:00	
8:30		8:30		8:30		8:30	
9:00		9:00		9:00		9:00	
9:30		9:30		9:30		9:30	
10:00		10:00		10:00		10:00	
10:30		10:30		10:30		10:30	
11:00		11:00		11:00		11:00	
11:30		11:30		11:30		11:30	
	I MEET MY GOALS		BUILDING MY DREAMS		NO EXCUSES		I AM AN AUTHOR
12:00		12:00		12:00		12:00	
12:30		12:30		12:30		12:30	
1:00		1:00		1:00		1:00	
1:30		1:30		1:30		1:30	
2:00		2:00		2:00		2:00	
2:30		2:30		2:30		2:30	
3:00		3:00		3:00		3:00	
3:30		3:30		3:30		3:30	
4:00		4:00		4:00		4:00	
4:30		4:30		4:30		4:30	
5:00		5:00		5:00		5:00	
5:30		5:30		5:30		5:30	
6:00		6:00		6:00		6:00	
6:30		6:30		6:30		6:30	
7:00		7:00		7:00		7:00	
7:30		7:30		7:30		7:30	
8:00		8:00		8:00		8:00	
WRITING PROGRESS		WRITING PROGRESS		WRITING PROGRESS		WRITING PROGRESS	

LOOKING AHEAD

Week Of

"Either write something worth reading or do something worth writing."
—Benjamin Franklin

PRIORITY GOALS

TO DO

DREAM GOALS

	MONDAY	TUESDAY	WEDNESDAY
	INTENTIONS	INTENTIONS	INTENTIONS
6:00			
6:30			
7:00			
7:30			
8:00			
8:30			
9:00			
9:30			
10:00			
10:30			
11:00			
11:30			
	I AM CREATIVE	MY WORDS MATTER	LIFE IS GOOD
12:00			
12:30			
1:00			
1:30			
2:00			
2:30			
3:00			
3:30			
4:00			
4:30			
5:00			
5:30			
6:00			
6:30			
7:00			
7:30			
8:00			
	WRITING PROGRESS	WRITING PROGRESS	WRITING PROGRESS
	GRATITUDES		

THURSDAY		FRIDAY		SATURDAY		SUNDAY	
INTENTIONS		INTENTIONS		INTENTIONS		INTENTIONS	
6:00		6:00		6:00		6:00	
6:30		6:30		6:30		6:30	
7:00		7:00		7:00		7:00	
7:30		7:30		7:30		7:30	
8:00		8:00		8:00		8:00	
8:30		8:30		8:30		8:30	
9:00		9:00		9:00		9:00	
9:30		9:30		9:30		9:30	
10:00		10:00		10:00		10:00	
10:30		10:30		10:30		10:30	
11:00		11:00		11:00		11:00	
11:30		11:30		11:30		11:30	
	I MEET MY GOALS		BUILDING MY DREAMS		NO EXCUSES		I AM AN AUTHOR
12:00		12:00		12:00		12:00	
12:30		12:30		12:30		12:30	
1:00		1:00		1:00		1:00	
1:30		1:30		1:30		1:30	
2:00		2:00		2:00		2:00	
2:30		2:30		2:30		2:30	
3:00		3:00		3:00		3:00	
3:30		3:30		3:30		3:30	
4:00		4:00		4:00		4:00	
4:30		4:30		4:30		4:30	
5:00		5:00		5:00		5:00	
5:30		5:30		5:30		5:30	
6:00		6:00		6:00		6:00	
6:30		6:30		6:30		6:30	
7:00		7:00		7:00		7:00	
7:30		7:30		7:30		7:30	
8:00		8:00		8:00		8:00	
WRITING PROGRESS		WRITING PROGRESS		WRITING PROGRESS		WRITING PROGRESS	

LOOKING AHEAD

Week Of

"If I waited for perfection, I would never write a word."
—Margaret Atwood

PRIORITY GOALS

TO DO

DREAM GOALS

	MONDAY		TUESDAY		WEDNESDAY
	INTENTIONS		INTENTIONS		INTENTIONS
6:00		6:00		6:00	
6:30		6:30		6:30	
7:00		7:00		7:00	
7:30		7:30		7:30	
8:00		8:00		8:00	
8:30		8:30		8:30	
9:00		9:00		9:00	
9:30		9:30		9:30	
10:00		10:00		10:00	
10:30		10:30		10:30	
11:00		11:00		11:00	
11:30		11:30		11:30	
	I AM CREATIVE		MY WORDS MATTER		LIFE IS GOOD
12:00		12:00		12:00	
12:30		12:30		12:30	
1:00		1:00		1:00	
1:30		1:30		1:30	
2:00		2:00		2:00	
2:30		2:30		2:30	
3:00		3:00		3:00	
3:30		3:30		3:30	
4:00		4:00		4:00	
4:30		4:30		4:30	
5:00		5:00		5:00	
5:30		5:30		5:30	
6:00		6:00		6:00	
6:30		6:30		6:30	
7:00		7:00		7:00	
7:30		7:30		7:30	
8:00		8:00		8:00	
WRITING PROGRESS		WRITING PROGRESS		WRITING PROGRESS	
GRATITUDES					

THURSDAY		FRIDAY		SATURDAY		SUNDAY	
INTENTIONS		INTENTIONS		INTENTIONS		INTENTIONS	
6:00		6:00		6:00		6:00	
6:30		6:30		6:30		6:30	
7:00		7:00		7:00		7:00	
7:30		7:30		7:30		7:30	
8:00		8:00		8:00		8:00	
8:30		8:30		8:30		8:30	
9:00		9:00		9:00		9:00	
9:30		9:30		9:30		9:30	
10:00		10:00		10:00		10:00	
10:30		10:30		10:30		10:30	
11:00		11:00		11:00		11:00	
11:30		11:30		11:30		11:30	
	I MEET MY GOALS		BUILDING MY DREAMS		NO EXCUSES		I AM AN AUTHOR
12:00		12:00		12:00		12:00	
12:30		12:30		12:30		12:30	
1:00		1:00		1:00		1:00	
1:30		1:30		1:30		1:30	
2:00		2:00		2:00		2:00	
2:30		2:30		2:30		2:30	
3:00		3:00		3:00		3:00	
3:30		3:30		3:30		3:30	
4:00		4:00		4:00		4:00	
4:30		4:30		4:30		4:30	
5:00		5:00		5:00		5:00	
5:30		5:30		5:30		5:30	
6:00		6:00		6:00		6:00	
6:30		6:30		6:30		6:30	
7:00		7:00		7:00		7:00	
7:30		7:30		7:30		7:30	
8:00		8:00		8:00		8:00	
WRITING PROGRESS		WRITING PROGRESS		WRITING PROGRESS		WRITING PROGRESS	

LOOKING AHEAD

Monthly Overview

How did my writing go this month?

Did I meet my writing and personal goals? Why or why not?

Am I happy with how I spent my time?
If not, what changes will I make?

What did I learn this month that proved helpful?

What was my biggest time/ energy waster this month? How can I eliminate it?

What have I been procrastinating on?

FIND A PLACE TO SCHEDULE IT NEXT MONTH

What goals do I want to meet next month?

Month:

MONDAY	TUESDAY	WEDNESDAY

This Month's Focus

Social Media Goals

THURSDAY	FRIDAY	SATURDAY	SUNDAY

 Sales / Releases / Queries

Week Of

If you wait for inspiration to write, you're not a writer, you're a waiter."
—Dan Poynter

PRIORITY GOALS

TO DO

DREAM GOALS

	MONDAY		TUESDAY		WEDNESDAY	
	INTENTIONS		INTENTIONS		INTENTIONS	
6:00		6:00		6:00		
6:30		6:30		6:30		
7:00		7:00		7:00		
7:30		7:30		7:30		
8:00		8:00		8:00		
8:30		8:30		8:30		
9:00		9:00		9:00		
9:30		9:30		9:30		
10:00		10:00		10:00		
10:30		10:30		10:30		
11:00		11:00		11:00		
11:30		11:30		11:30		
	I AM CREATIVE		MY WORDS MATTER		LIFE IS GOOD	
12:00		12:00		12:00		
12:30		12:30		12:30		
1:00		1:00		1:00		
1:30		1:30		1:30		
2:00		2:00		2:00		
2:30		2:30		2:30		
3:00		3:00		3:00		
3:30		3:30		3:30		
4:00		4:00		4:00		
4:30		4:30		4:30		
5:00		5:00		5:00		
5:30		5:30		5:30		
6:00		6:00		6:00		
6:30		6:30		6:30		
7:00		7:00		7:00		
7:30		7:30		7:30		
8:00		8:00		8:00		
WRITING PROGRESS		WRITING PROGRESS		WRITING PROGRESS		
GRATITUDES						

THURSDAY		FRIDAY		SATURDAY		SUNDAY	
INTENTIONS		INTENTIONS		INTENTIONS		INTENTIONS	
6:00		6:00		6:00		6:00	
6:30		6:30		6:30		6:30	
7:00		7:00		7:00		7:00	
7:30		7:30		7:30		7:30	
8:00		8:00		8:00		8:00	
8:30		8:30		8:30		8:30	
9:00		9:00		9:00		9:00	
9:30		9:30		9:30		9:30	
10:00		10:00		10:00		10:00	
10:30		10:30		10:30		10:30	
11:00		11:00		11:00		11:00	
11:30		11:30		11:30		11:30	
	I MEET MY GOALS		BUILDING MY DREAMS		NO EXCUSES		I AM AN AUTHOR
12:00		12:00		12:00		12:00	
12:30		12:30		12:30		12:30	
1:00		1:00		1:00		1:00	
1:30		1:30		1:30		1:30	
2:00		2:00		2:00		2:00	
2:30		2:30		2:30		2:30	
3:00		3:00		3:00		3:00	
3:30		3:30		3:30		3:30	
4:00		4:00		4:00		4:00	
4:30		4:30		4:30		4:30	
5:00		5:00		5:00		5:00	
5:30		5:30		5:30		5:30	
6:00		6:00		6:00		6:00	
6:30		6:30		6:30		6:30	
7:00		7:00		7:00		7:00	
7:30		7:30		7:30		7:30	
8:00		8:00		8:00		8:00	
WRITING PROGRESS		WRITING PROGRESS		WRITING PROGRESS		WRITING PROGRESS	

LOOKING AHEAD

Week Of

"We need to do a better job of putting ourselves higher on our own 'to-do' list."
—Michelle Obama

PRIORITY GOALS

TO DO

DREAM GOALS

	MONDAY		TUESDAY		WEDNESDAY
	INTENTIONS		INTENTIONS		INTENTIONS
6:00		6:00		6:00	
6:30		6:30		6:30	
7:00		7:00		7:00	
7:30		7:30		7:30	
8:00		8:00		8:00	
8:30		8:30		8:30	
9:00		9:00		9:00	
9:30		9:30		9:30	
10:00		10:00		10:00	
10:30		10:30		10:30	
11:00		11:00		11:00	
11:30		11:30		11:30	
	I AM CREATIVE		MY WORDS MATTER		LIFE IS GOOD
12:00		12:00		12:00	
12:30		12:30		12:30	
1:00		1:00		1:00	
1:30		1:30		1:30	
2:00		2:00		2:00	
2:30		2:30		2:30	
3:00		3:00		3:00	
3:30		3:30		3:30	
4:00		4:00		4:00	
4:30		4:30		4:30	
5:00		5:00		5:00	
5:30		5:30		5:30	
6:00		6:00		6:00	
6:30		6:30		6:30	
7:00		7:00		7:00	
7:30		7:30		7:30	
8:00		8:00		8:00	
WRITING PROGRESS		WRITING PROGRESS		WRITING PROGRESS	
GRATITUDES					

THURSDAY		FRIDAY		SATURDAY		SUNDAY	
INTENTIONS		INTENTIONS		INTENTIONS		INTENTIONS	
6:00		6:00		6:00		6:00	
6:30		6:30		6:30		6:30	
7:00		7:00		7:00		7:00	
7:30		7:30		7:30		7:30	
8:00		8:00		8:00		8:00	
8:30		8:30		8:30		8:30	
9:00		9:00		9:00		9:00	
9:30		9:30		9:30		9:30	
10:00		10:00		10:00		10:00	
10:30		10:30		10:30		10:30	
11:00		11:00		11:00		11:00	
11:30		11:30		11:30		11:30	
	I MEET MY GOALS		BUILDING MY DREAMS		NO EXCUSES		I AM AN AUTHOR
12:00		12:00		12:00		12:00	
12:30		12:30		12:30		12:30	
1:00		1:00		1:00		1:00	
1:30		1:30		1:30		1:30	
2:00		2:00		2:00		2:00	
2:30		2:30		2:30		2:30	
3:00		3:00		3:00		3:00	
3:30		3:30		3:30		3:30	
4:00		4:00		4:00		4:00	
4:30		4:30		4:30		4:30	
5:00		5:00		5:00		5:00	
5:30		5:30		5:30		5:30	
6:00		6:00		6:00		6:00	
6:30		6:30		6:30		6:30	
7:00		7:00		7:00		7:00	
7:30		7:30		7:30		7:30	
8:00		8:00		8:00		8:00	
WRITING PROGRESS		WRITING PROGRESS		WRITING PROGRESS		WRITING PROGRESS	

LOOKING AHEAD

Week Of

"Your journey is a book waiting to be written."
—Demi Stevens

PRIORITY GOALS

TO DO

DREAM GOALS

	MONDAY		TUESDAY		WEDNESDAY
	INTENTIONS		**INTENTIONS**		**INTENTIONS**
6:00		6:00		6:00	
6:30		6:30		6:30	
7:00		7:00		7:00	
7:30		7:30		7:30	
8:00		8:00		8:00	
8:30		8:30		8:30	
9:00		9:00		9:00	
9:30		9:30		9:30	
10:00		10:00		10:00	
10:30		10:30		10:30	
11:00		11:00		11:00	
11:30		11:30		11:30	
	I AM CREATIVE		**MY WORDS MATTER**		**LIFE IS GOOD**
12:00		12:00		12:00	
12:30		12:30		12:30	
1:00		1:00		1:00	
1:30		1:30		1:30	
2:00		2:00		2:00	
2:30		2:30		2:30	
3:00		3:00		3:00	
3:30		3:30		3:30	
4:00		4:00		4:00	
4:30		4:30		4:30	
5:00		5:00		5:00	
5:30		5:30		5:30	
6:00		6:00		6:00	
6:30		6:30		6:30	
7:00		7:00		7:00	
7:30		7:30		7:30	
8:00		8:00		8:00	
WRITING PROGRESS		**WRITING PROGRESS**		**WRITING PROGRESS**	

GRATITUDES

THURSDAY		FRIDAY		SATURDAY		SUNDAY	
INTENTIONS		INTENTIONS		INTENTIONS		INTENTIONS	
6:00		6:00		6:00		6:00	
6:30		6:30		6:30		6:30	
7:00		7:00		7:00		7:00	
7:30		7:30		7:30		7:30	
8:00		8:00		8:00		8:00	
8:30		8:30		8:30		8:30	
9:00		9:00		9:00		9:00	
9:30		9:30		9:30		9:30	
10:00		10:00		10:00		10:00	
10:30		10:30		10:30		10:30	
11:00		11:00		11:00		11:00	
11:30		11:30		11:30		11:30	
	I MEET MY GOALS		BUILDING MY DREAMS		NO EXCUSES		I AM AN AUTHOR
12:00		12:00		12:00		12:00	
12:30		12:30		12:30		12:30	
1:00		1:00		1:00		1:00	
1:30		1:30		1:30		1:30	
2:00		2:00		2:00		2:00	
2:30		2:30		2:30		2:30	
3:00		3:00		3:00		3:00	
3:30		3:30		3:30		3:30	
4:00		4:00		4:00		4:00	
4:30		4:30		4:30		4:30	
5:00		5:00		5:00		5:00	
5:30		5:30		5:30		5:30	
6:00		6:00		6:00		6:00	
6:30		6:30		6:30		6:30	
7:00		7:00		7:00		7:00	
7:30		7:30		7:30		7:30	
8:00		8:00		8:00		8:00	
WRITING PROGRESS		WRITING PROGRESS		WRITING PROGRESS		WRITING PROGRESS	

LOOKING AHEAD

Week Of

"We are what we repeatedly do. Excellence, therefore, is not an act, but a habit."
—Aristotle

PRIORITY GOALS

TO DO

DREAM GOALS

	MONDAY	TUESDAY	WEDNESDAY
	INTENTIONS	INTENTIONS	INTENTIONS
6:00			
6:30			
7:00			
7:30			
8:00			
8:30			
9:00			
9:30			
10:00			
10:30			
11:00			
11:30			
	I AM CREATIVE	MY WORDS MATTER	LIFE IS GOOD
12:00			
12:30			
1:00			
1:30			
2:00			
2:30			
3:00			
3:30			
4:00			
4:30			
5:00			
5:30			
6:00			
6:30			
7:00			
7:30			
8:00			
WRITING PROGRESS	WRITING PROGRESS	WRITING PROGRESS

GRATITUDES

THURSDAY		FRIDAY		SATURDAY		SUNDAY	
INTENTIONS		INTENTIONS		INTENTIONS		INTENTIONS	
6:00		6:00		6:00		6:00	
6:30		6:30		6:30		6:30	
7:00		7:00		7:00		7:00	
7:30		7:30		7:30		7:30	
8:00		8:00		8:00		8:00	
8:30		8:30		8:30		8:30	
9:00		9:00		9:00		9:00	
9:30		9:30		9:30		9:30	
10:00		10:00		10:00		10:00	
10:30		10:30		10:30		10:30	
11:00		11:00		11:00		11:00	
11:30		11:30		11:30		11:30	
	I MEET MY GOALS		BUILDING MY DREAMS		NO EXCUSES		I AM AN AUTHOR
12:00		12:00		12:00		12:00	
12:30		12:30		12:30		12:30	
1:00		1:00		1:00		1:00	
1:30		1:30		1:30		1:30	
2:00		2:00		2:00		2:00	
2:30		2:30		2:30		2:30	
3:00		3:00		3:00		3:00	
3:30		3:30		3:30		3:30	
4:00		4:00		4:00		4:00	
4:30		4:30		4:30		4:30	
5:00		5:00		5:00		5:00	
5:30		5:30		5:30		5:30	
6:00		6:00		6:00		6:00	
6:30		6:30		6:30		6:30	
7:00		7:00		7:00		7:00	
7:30		7:30		7:30		7:30	
8:00		8:00		8:00		8:00	
WRITING PROGRESS		WRITING PROGRESS		WRITING PROGRESS		WRITING PROGRESS	

LOOKING AHEAD

Quarterly Overview

**Am I still on target with my yearly goals?
Or have I chosen a new path?**

What interfered with my progress?

What can I do next quarter to eliminate these obstacles?

What do I need to let go of this coming quarter?

What happened this quarter that I need to reframe positively?

How do my work and activities reflect the yearly word I chose?

What do I hope to accomplish next quarter?

# Month:

MONDAY	TUESDAY	WEDNESDAY

This Month's Focus

Social Media Goals

THURSDAY	FRIDAY	SATURDAY	SUNDAY

 Sales / Releases / Queries

Week Of

"Great writers aren't great first drafters. They're great rewriters."
—Andrew Bennett

PRIORITY GOALS

TO DO

DREAM GOALS

	MONDAY		TUESDAY		WEDNESDAY
	INTENTIONS		INTENTIONS		INTENTIONS
6:00		6:00		6:00	
6:30		6:30		6:30	
7:00		7:00		7:00	
7:30		7:30		7:30	
8:00		8:00		8:00	
8:30		8:30		8:30	
9:00		9:00		9:00	
9:30		9:30		9:30	
10:00		10:00		10:00	
10:30		10:30		10:30	
11:00		11:00		11:00	
11:30		11:30		11:30	
	I AM CREATIVE		MY WORDS MATTER		LIFE IS GOOD
12:00		12:00		12:00	
12:30		12:30		12:30	
1:00		1:00		1:00	
1:30		1:30		1:30	
2:00		2:00		2:00	
2:30		2:30		2:30	
3:00		3:00		3:00	
3:30		3:30		3:30	
4:00		4:00		4:00	
4:30		4:30		4:30	
5:00		5:00		5:00	
5:30		5:30		5:30	
6:00		6:00		6:00	
6:30		6:30		6:30	
7:00		7:00		7:00	
7:30		7:30		7:30	
8:00		8:00		8:00	
WRITING PROGRESS		WRITING PROGRESS		WRITING PROGRESS	

GRATITUDES

THURSDAY		FRIDAY		SATURDAY		SUNDAY	
INTENTIONS		INTENTIONS		INTENTIONS		INTENTIONS	
6:00		6:00		6:00		6:00	
6:30		6:30		6:30		6:30	
7:00		7:00		7:00		7:00	
7:30		7:30		7:30		7:30	
8:00		8:00		8:00		8:00	
8:30		8:30		8:30		8:30	
9:00		9:00		9:00		9:00	
9:30		9:30		9:30		9:30	
10:00		10:00		10:00		10:00	
10:30		10:30		10:30		10:30	
11:00		11:00		11:00		11:00	
11:30		11:30		11:30		11:30	
	I MEET MY GOALS		BUILDING MY DREAMS		NO EXCUSES		I AM AN AUTHOR
12:00		12:00		12:00		12:00	
12:30		12:30		12:30		12:30	
1:00		1:00		1:00		1:00	
1:30		1:30		1:30		1:30	
2:00		2:00		2:00		2:00	
2:30		2:30		2:30		2:30	
3:00		3:00		3:00		3:00	
3:30		3:30		3:30		3:30	
4:00		4:00		4:00		4:00	
4:30		4:30		4:30		4:30	
5:00		5:00		5:00		5:00	
5:30		5:30		5:30		5:30	
6:00		6:00		6:00		6:00	
6:30		6:30		6:30		6:30	
7:00		7:00		7:00		7:00	
7:30		7:30		7:30		7:30	
8:00		8:00		8:00		8:00	
WRITING PROGRESS		WRITING PROGRESS		WRITING PROGRESS		WRITING PROGRESS	

LOOKING AHEAD

Week Of

"Better three hours too soon than a minute too late."
—William Shakespeare

PRIORITY GOALS

TO DO

DREAM GOALS

	MONDAY		TUESDAY		WEDNESDAY
	INTENTIONS		INTENTIONS		INTENTIONS
6:00		6:00		6:00	
6:30		6:30		6:30	
7:00		7:00		7:00	
7:30		7:30		7:30	
8:00		8:00		8:00	
8:30		8:30		8:30	
9:00		9:00		9:00	
9:30		9:30		9:30	
10:00		10:00		10:00	
10:30		10:30		10:30	
11:00		11:00		11:00	
11:30		11:30		11:30	
	I AM CREATIVE		MY WORDS MATTER		LIFE IS GOOD
12:00		12:00		12:00	
12:30		12:30		12:30	
1:00		1:00		1:00	
1:30		1:30		1:30	
2:00		2:00		2:00	
2:30		2:30		2:30	
3:00		3:00		3:00	
3:30		3:30		3:30	
4:00		4:00		4:00	
4:30		4:30		4:30	
5:00		5:00		5:00	
5:30		5:30		5:30	
6:00		6:00		6:00	
6:30		6:30		6:30	
7:00		7:00		7:00	
7:30		7:30		7:30	
8:00		8:00		8:00	
WRITING PROGRESS		WRITING PROGRESS		WRITING PROGRESS	
GRATITUDES					

THURSDAY		FRIDAY		SATURDAY		SUNDAY	
INTENTIONS		INTENTIONS		INTENTIONS		INTENTIONS	
6:00		6:00		6:00		6:00	
6:30		6:30		6:30		6:30	
7:00		7:00		7:00		7:00	
7:30		7:30		7:30		7:30	
8:00		8:00		8:00		8:00	
8:30		8:30		8:30		8:30	
9:00		9:00		9:00		9:00	
9:30		9:30		9:30		9:30	
10:00		10:00		10:00		10:00	
10:30		10:30		10:30		10:30	
11:00		11:00		11:00		11:00	
11:30		11:30		11:30		11:30	
	I MEET MY GOALS		BUILDING MY DREAMS		NO EXCUSES		I AM AN AUTHOR
12:00		12:00		12:00		12:00	
12:30		12:30		12:30		12:30	
1:00		1:00		1:00		1:00	
1:30		1:30		1:30		1:30	
2:00		2:00		2:00		2:00	
2:30		2:30		2:30		2:30	
3:00		3:00		3:00		3:00	
3:30		3:30		3:30		3:30	
4:00		4:00		4:00		4:00	
4:30		4:30		4:30		4:30	
5:00		5:00		5:00		5:00	
5:30		5:30		5:30		5:30	
6:00		6:00		6:00		6:00	
6:30		6:30		6:30		6:30	
7:00		7:00		7:00		7:00	
7:30		7:30		7:30		7:30	
8:00		8:00		8:00		8:00	
WRITING PROGRESS		WRITING PROGRESS		WRITING PROGRESS		WRITING PROGRESS	

LOOKING AHEAD

Week Of

Three paragraphs a day keeps the writer's block away.

PRIORITY GOALS

TO DO

DREAM GOALS

	MONDAY		TUESDAY		WEDNESDAY	
	INTENTIONS		INTENTIONS		INTENTIONS	
6:00		6:00		6:00		
6:30		6:30		6:30		
7:00		7:00		7:00		
7:30		7:30		7:30		
8:00		8:00		8:00		
8:30		8:30		8:30		
9:00		9:00		9:00		
9:30		9:30		9:30		
10:00		10:00		10:00		
10:30		10:30		10:30		
11:00		11:00		11:00		
11:30		11:30		11:30		
	I AM CREATIVE		MY WORDS MATTER		LIFE IS GOOD	
12:00		12:00		12:00		
12:30		12:30		12:30		
1:00		1:00		1:00		
1:30		1:30		1:30		
2:00		2:00		2:00		
2:30		2:30		2:30		
3:00		3:00		3:00		
3:30		3:30		3:30		
4:00		4:00		4:00		
4:30		4:30		4:30		
5:00		5:00		5:00		
5:30		5:30		5:30		
6:00		6:00		6:00		
6:30		6:30		6:30		
7:00		7:00		7:00		
7:30		7:30		7:30		
8:00		8:00		8:00		
WRITING PROGRESS		WRITING PROGRESS		WRITING PROGRESS		
GRATITUDES						

THURSDAY		FRIDAY		SATURDAY		SUNDAY	
INTENTIONS		INTENTIONS		INTENTIONS		INTENTIONS	
6:00		6:00		6:00		6:00	
6:30		6:30		6:30		6:30	
7:00		7:00		7:00		7:00	
7:30		7:30		7:30		7:30	
8:00		8:00		8:00		8:00	
8:30		8:30		8:30		8:30	
9:00		9:00		9:00		9:00	
9:30		9:30		9:30		9:30	
10:00		10:00		10:00		10:00	
10:30		10:30		10:30		10:30	
11:00		11:00		11:00		11:00	
11:30		11:30		11:30		11:30	
	I MEET MY GOALS		BUILDING MY DREAMS		NO EXCUSES		I AM AN AUTHOR
12:00		12:00		12:00		12:00	
12:30		12:30		12:30		12:30	
1:00		1:00		1:00		1:00	
1:30		1:30		1:30		1:30	
2:00		2:00		2:00		2:00	
2:30		2:30		2:30		2:30	
3:00		3:00		3:00		3:00	
3:30		3:30		3:30		3:30	
4:00		4:00		4:00		4:00	
4:30		4:30		4:30		4:30	
5:00		5:00		5:00		5:00	
5:30		5:30		5:30		5:30	
6:00		6:00		6:00		6:00	
6:30		6:30		6:30		6:30	
7:00		7:00		7:00		7:00	
7:30		7:30		7:30		7:30	
8:00		8:00		8:00		8:00	
WRITING PROGRESS		WRITING PROGRESS		WRITING PROGRESS		WRITING PROGRESS	

LOOKING AHEAD

Week Of

You know all these things you've wanted to do?

You should go DO them!

PRIORITY GOALS

TO DO

DREAM GOALS

	MONDAY		TUESDAY		WEDNESDAY
	INTENTIONS		INTENTIONS		INTENTIONS
6:00		6:00		6:00	
6:30		6:30		6:30	
7:00		7:00		7:00	
7:30		7:30		7:30	
8:00		8:00		8:00	
8:30		8:30		8:30	
9:00		9:00		9:00	
9:30		9:30		9:30	
10:00		10:00		10:00	
10:30		10:30		10:30	
11:00		11:00		11:00	
11:30		11:30		11:30	
	I AM CREATIVE		MY WORDS MATTER		LIFE IS GOOD
12:00		12:00		12:00	
12:30		12:30		12:30	
1:00		1:00		1:00	
1:30		1:30		1:30	
2:00		2:00		2:00	
2:30		2:30		2:30	
3:00		3:00		3:00	
3:30		3:30		3:30	
4:00		4:00		4:00	
4:30		4:30		4:30	
5:00		5:00		5:00	
5:30		5:30		5:30	
6:00		6:00		6:00	
6:30		6:30		6:30	
7:00		7:00		7:00	
7:30		7:30		7:30	
8:00		8:00		8:00	
WRITING PROGRESS		WRITING PROGRESS		WRITING PROGRESS	
GRATITUDES					

THURSDAY		FRIDAY		SATURDAY		SUNDAY	
INTENTIONS		INTENTIONS		INTENTIONS		INTENTIONS	
6:00		6:00		6:00		6:00	
6:30		6:30		6:30		6:30	
7:00		7:00		7:00		7:00	
7:30		7:30		7:30		7:30	
8:00		8:00		8:00		8:00	
8:30		8:30		8:30		8:30	
9:00		9:00		9:00		9:00	
9:30		9:30		9:30		9:30	
10:00		10:00		10:00		10:00	
10:30		10:30		10:30		10:30	
11:00		11:00		11:00		11:00	
11:30		11:30		11:30		11:30	
	I MEET MY GOALS		BUILDING MY DREAMS		NO EXCUSES		I AM AN AUTHOR
12:00		12:00		12:00		12:00	
12:30		12:30		12:30		12:30	
1:00		1:00		1:00		1:00	
1:30		1:30		1:30		1:30	
2:00		2:00		2:00		2:00	
2:30		2:30		2:30		2:30	
3:00		3:00		3:00		3:00	
3:30		3:30		3:30		3:30	
4:00		4:00		4:00		4:00	
4:30		4:30		4:30		4:30	
5:00		5:00		5:00		5:00	
5:30		5:30		5:30		5:30	
6:00		6:00		6:00		6:00	
6:30		6:30		6:30		6:30	
7:00		7:00		7:00		7:00	
7:30		7:30		7:30		7:30	
8:00		8:00		8:00		8:00	
WRITING PROGRESS		WRITING PROGRESS		WRITING PROGRESS		WRITING PROGRESS	

LOOKING AHEAD

Week Of

"Don't worry that someone will steal your stuff. Worry if no one tries to steal your stuff."
—Demi Stevens

PRIORITY GOALS

TO DO

DREAM GOALS

	MONDAY		TUESDAY		WEDNESDAY
	INTENTIONS		INTENTIONS		INTENTIONS
6:00		6:00		6:00	
6:30		6:30		6:30	
7:00		7:00		7:00	
7:30		7:30		7:30	
8:00		8:00		8:00	
8:30		8:30		8:30	
9:00		9:00		9:00	
9:30		9:30		9:30	
10:00		10:00		10:00	
10:30		10:30		10:30	
11:00		11:00		11:00	
11:30		11:30		11:30	
	I AM CREATIVE		MY WORDS MATTER		LIFE IS GOOD
12:00		12:00		12:00	
12:30		12:30		12:30	
1:00		1:00		1:00	
1:30		1:30		1:30	
2:00		2:00		2:00	
2:30		2:30		2:30	
3:00		3:00		3:00	
3:30		3:30		3:30	
4:00		4:00		4:00	
4:30		4:30		4:30	
5:00		5:00		5:00	
5:30		5:30		5:30	
6:00		6:00		6:00	
6:30		6:30		6:30	
7:00		7:00		7:00	
7:30		7:30		7:30	
8:00		8:00		8:00	
WRITING PROGRESS		WRITING PROGRESS		WRITING PROGRESS	
GRATITUDES					

THURSDAY		FRIDAY		SATURDAY		SUNDAY	
INTENTIONS		INTENTIONS		INTENTIONS		INTENTIONS	
6:00		6:00		6:00		6:00	
6:30		6:30		6:30		6:30	
7:00		7:00		7:00		7:00	
7:30		7:30		7:30		7:30	
8:00		8:00		8:00		8:00	
8:30		8:30		8:30		8:30	
9:00		9:00		9:00		9:00	
9:30		9:30		9:30		9:30	
10:00		10:00		10:00		10:00	
10:30		10:30		10:30		10:30	
11:00		11:00		11:00		11:00	
11:30		11:30		11:30		11:30	
	I MEET MY GOALS		BUILDING MY DREAMS		NO EXCUSES		I AM AN AUTHOR
12:00		12:00		12:00		12:00	
12:30		12:30		12:30		12:30	
1:00		1:00		1:00		1:00	
1:30		1:30		1:30		1:30	
2:00		2:00		2:00		2:00	
2:30		2:30		2:30		2:30	
3:00		3:00		3:00		3:00	
3:30		3:30		3:30		3:30	
4:00		4:00		4:00		4:00	
4:30		4:30		4:30		4:30	
5:00		5:00		5:00		5:00	
5:30		5:30		5:30		5:30	
6:00		6:00		6:00		6:00	
6:30		6:30		6:30		6:30	
7:00		7:00		7:00		7:00	
7:30		7:30		7:30		7:30	
8:00		8:00		8:00		8:00	
WRITING PROGRESS		WRITING PROGRESS		WRITING PROGRESS		WRITING PROGRESS	

LOOKING AHEAD

Monthly Overview

How did my writing go this month?

Did I meet my writing and personal goals? Why or why not?

Am I happy with how I spent my time? If not, what changes will I make?

What did I learn this month that proved helpful?

What was my biggest time/ energy waster this month? How can I eliminate it?

What have I been procrastinating on?

FIND A PLACE TO SCHEDULE IT NEXT MONTH

What goals do I want to meet next month?

Month:

MONDAY	TUESDAY	WEDNESDAY

This Month's Focus

Social Media Goals

THURSDAY	FRIDAY	SATURDAY	SUNDAY

 Sales / Releases / Queries

Week Of

"If you're not making mistakes, then you're not making decisions."
—Catherine Cook

PRIORITY GOALS

TO DO

DREAM GOALS

	MONDAY		TUESDAY		WEDNESDAY
	INTENTIONS		INTENTIONS		INTENTIONS
6:00		6:00		6:00	
6:30		6:30		6:30	
7:00		7:00		7:00	
7:30		7:30		7:30	
8:00		8:00		8:00	
8:30		8:30		8:30	
9:00		9:00		9:00	
9:30		9:30		9:30	
10:00		10:00		10:00	
10:30		10:30		10:30	
11:00		11:00		11:00	
11:30		11:30		11:30	
	I AM CREATIVE		MY WORDS MATTER		LIFE IS GOOD
12:00		12:00		12:00	
12:30		12:30		12:30	
1:00		1:00		1:00	
1:30		1:30		1:30	
2:00		2:00		2:00	
2:30		2:30		2:30	
3:00		3:00		3:00	
3:30		3:30		3:30	
4:00		4:00		4:00	
4:30		4:30		4:30	
5:00		5:00		5:00	
5:30		5:30		5:30	
6:00		6:00		6:00	
6:30		6:30		6:30	
7:00		7:00		7:00	
7:30		7:30		7:30	
8:00		8:00		8:00	
WRITING PROGRESS		WRITING PROGRESS		WRITING PROGRESS	
GRATITUDES					

THURSDAY		FRIDAY		SATURDAY		SUNDAY	
INTENTIONS		INTENTIONS		INTENTIONS		INTENTIONS	
6:00		6:00		6:00		6:00	
6:30		6:30		6:30		6:30	
7:00		7:00		7:00		7:00	
7:30		7:30		7:30		7:30	
8:00		8:00		8:00		8:00	
8:30		8:30		8:30		8:30	
9:00		9:00		9:00		9:00	
9:30		9:30		9:30		9:30	
10:00		10:00		10:00		10:00	
10:30		10:30		10:30		10:30	
11:00		11:00		11:00		11:00	
11:30		11:30		11:30		11:30	
	I MEET MY GOALS		BUILDING MY DREAMS		NO EXCUSES		I AM AN AUTHOR
12:00		12:00		12:00		12:00	
12:30		12:30		12:30		12:30	
1:00		1:00		1:00		1:00	
1:30		1:30		1:30		1:30	
2:00		2:00		2:00		2:00	
2:30		2:30		2:30		2:30	
3:00		3:00		3:00		3:00	
3:30		3:30		3:30		3:30	
4:00		4:00		4:00		4:00	
4:30		4:30		4:30		4:30	
5:00		5:00		5:00		5:00	
5:30		5:30		5:30		5:30	
6:00		6:00		6:00		6:00	
6:30		6:30		6:30		6:30	
7:00		7:00		7:00		7:00	
7:30		7:30		7:30		7:30	
8:00		8:00		8:00		8:00	
WRITING PROGRESS		WRITING PROGRESS		WRITING PROGRESS		WRITING PROGRESS	

LOOKING AHEAD

Week Of

"Good fiction's job is to comfort the disturbed and disturb the comfortable."
—David Foster Wallace

PRIORITY GOALS

TO DO

DREAM GOALS

	MONDAY		TUESDAY		WEDNESDAY
	INTENTIONS		INTENTIONS		INTENTIONS
6:00		6:00		6:00	
6:30		6:30		6:30	
7:00		7:00		7:00	
7:30		7:30		7:30	
8:00		8:00		8:00	
8:30		8:30		8:30	
9:00		9:00		9:00	
9:30		9:30		9:30	
10:00		10:00		10:00	
10:30		10:30		10:30	
11:00		11:00		11:00	
11:30		11:30		11:30	
	I AM CREATIVE		MY WORDS MATTER		LIFE IS GOOD
12:00		12:00		12:00	
12:30		12:30		12:30	
1:00		1:00		1:00	
1:30		1:30		1:30	
2:00		2:00		2:00	
2:30		2:30		2:30	
3:00		3:00		3:00	
3:30		3:30		3:30	
4:00		4:00		4:00	
4:30		4:30		4:30	
5:00		5:00		5:00	
5:30		5:30		5:30	
6:00		6:00		6:00	
6:30		6:30		6:30	
7:00		7:00		7:00	
7:30		7:30		7:30	
8:00		8:00		8:00	
WRITING PROGRESS		WRITING PROGRESS		WRITING PROGRESS	
GRATITUDES					

THURSDAY		FRIDAY		SATURDAY		SUNDAY	
INTENTIONS		INTENTIONS		INTENTIONS		INTENTIONS	
6:00		6:00		6:00		6:00	
6:30		6:30		6:30		6:30	
7:00		7:00		7:00		7:00	
7:30		7:30		7:30		7:30	
8:00		8:00		8:00		8:00	
8:30		8:30		8:30		8:30	
9:00		9:00		9:00		9:00	
9:30		9:30		9:30		9:30	
10:00		10:00		10:00		10:00	
10:30		10:30		10:30		10:30	
11:00		11:00		11:00		11:00	
11:30		11:30		11:30		11:30	
	I MEET MY GOALS		BUILDING MY DREAMS		NO EXCUSES		I AM AN AUTHOR
12:00		12:00		12:00		12:00	
12:30		12:30		12:30		12:30	
1:00		1:00		1:00		1:00	
1:30		1:30		1:30		1:30	
2:00		2:00		2:00		2:00	
2:30		2:30		2:30		2:30	
3:00		3:00		3:00		3:00	
3:30		3:30		3:30		3:30	
4:00		4:00		4:00		4:00	
4:30		4:30		4:30		4:30	
5:00		5:00		5:00		5:00	
5:30		5:30		5:30		5:30	
6:00		6:00		6:00		6:00	
6:30		6:30		6:30		6:30	
7:00		7:00		7:00		7:00	
7:30		7:30		7:30		7:30	
8:00		8:00		8:00		8:00	
WRITING PROGRESS		WRITING PROGRESS		WRITING PROGRESS		WRITING PROGRESS	

LOOKING AHEAD

Week Of

"Start by doing what's necessary, then do what's possible, and suddenly you are doing the impossible."
—St. Francis of Assisi

PRIORITY GOALS

TO DO

DREAM GOALS

	MONDAY	TUESDAY	WEDNESDAY
	INTENTIONS	INTENTIONS	INTENTIONS
6:00			
6:30			
7:00			
7:30			
8:00			
8:30			
9:00			
9:30			
10:00			
10:30			
11:00			
11:30			
	I AM CREATIVE	MY WORDS MATTER	LIFE IS GOOD
12:00			
12:30			
1:00			
1:30			
2:00			
2:30			
3:00			
3:30			
4:00			
4:30			
5:00			
5:30			
6:00			
6:30			
7:00			
7:30			
8:00			
	WRITING PROGRESS	WRITING PROGRESS	WRITING PROGRESS

GRATITUDES

THURSDAY		FRIDAY		SATURDAY		SUNDAY	
INTENTIONS		INTENTIONS		INTENTIONS		INTENTIONS	
6:00		6:00		6:00		6:00	
6:30		6:30		6:30		6:30	
7:00		7:00		7:00		7:00	
7:30		7:30		7:30		7:30	
8:00		8:00		8:00		8:00	
8:30		8:30		8:30		8:30	
9:00		9:00		9:00		9:00	
9:30		9:30		9:30		9:30	
10:00		10:00		10:00		10:00	
10:30		10:30		10:30		10:30	
11:00		11:00		11:00		11:00	
11:30		11:30		11:30		11:30	
	I MEET MY GOALS		BUILDING MY DREAMS		NO EXCUSES		I AM AN AUTHOR
12:00		12:00		12:00		12:00	
12:30		12:30		12:30		12:30	
1:00		1:00		1:00		1:00	
1:30		1:30		1:30		1:30	
2:00		2:00		2:00		2:00	
2:30		2:30		2:30		2:30	
3:00		3:00		3:00		3:00	
3:30		3:30		3:30		3:30	
4:00		4:00		4:00		4:00	
4:30		4:30		4:30		4:30	
5:00		5:00		5:00		5:00	
5:30		5:30		5:30		5:30	
6:00		6:00		6:00		6:00	
6:30		6:30		6:30		6:30	
7:00		7:00		7:00		7:00	
7:30		7:30		7:30		7:30	
8:00		8:00		8:00		8:00	
WRITING PROGRESS		WRITING PROGRESS		WRITING PROGRESS		WRITING PROGRESS	

LOOKING AHEAD

Week Of

"Always read something that will make you look good if you die in the middle of it."
—P.J. O'Rourke

PRIORITY GOALS

TO DO

DREAM GOALS

	MONDAY		TUESDAY		WEDNESDAY
	INTENTIONS		INTENTIONS		INTENTIONS
6:00		6:00		6:00	
6:30		6:30		6:30	
7:00		7:00		7:00	
7:30		7:30		7:30	
8:00		8:00		8:00	
8:30		8:30		8:30	
9:00		9:00		9:00	
9:30		9:30		9:30	
10:00		10:00		10:00	
10:30		10:30		10:30	
11:00		11:00		11:00	
11:30		11:30		11:30	
	I AM CREATIVE		MY WORDS MATTER		LIFE IS GOOD
12:00		12:00		12:00	
12:30		12:30		12:30	
1:00		1:00		1:00	
1:30		1:30		1:30	
2:00		2:00		2:00	
2:30		2:30		2:30	
3:00		3:00		3:00	
3:30		3:30		3:30	
4:00		4:00		4:00	
4:30		4:30		4:30	
5:00		5:00		5:00	
5:30		5:30		5:30	
6:00		6:00		6:00	
6:30		6:30		6:30	
7:00		7:00		7:00	
7:30		7:30		7:30	
8:00		8:00		8:00	
WRITING PROGRESS		WRITING PROGRESS		WRITING PROGRESS	
GRATITUDES					

THURSDAY		FRIDAY		SATURDAY		SUNDAY	
INTENTIONS		INTENTIONS		INTENTIONS		INTENTIONS	
6:00		6:00		6:00		6:00	
6:30		6:30		6:30		6:30	
7:00		7:00		7:00		7:00	
7:30		7:30		7:30		7:30	
8:00		8:00		8:00		8:00	
8:30		8:30		8:30		8:30	
9:00		9:00		9:00		9:00	
9:30		9:30		9:30		9:30	
10:00		10:00		10:00		10:00	
10:30		10:30		10:30		10:30	
11:00		11:00		11:00		11:00	
11:30		11:30		11:30		11:30	
	I MEET MY GOALS		BUILDING MY DREAMS		NO EXCUSES		I AM AN AUTHOR
12:00		12:00		12:00		12:00	
12:30		12:30		12:30		12:30	
1:00		1:00		1:00		1:00	
1:30		1:30		1:30		1:30	
2:00		2:00		2:00		2:00	
2:30		2:30		2:30		2:30	
3:00		3:00		3:00		3:00	
3:30		3:30		3:30		3:30	
4:00		4:00		4:00		4:00	
4:30		4:30		4:30		4:30	
5:00		5:00		5:00		5:00	
5:30		5:30		5:30		5:30	
6:00		6:00		6:00		6:00	
6:30		6:30		6:30		6:30	
7:00		7:00		7:00		7:00	
7:30		7:30		7:30		7:30	
8:00		8:00		8:00		8:00	
WRITING PROGRESS		WRITING PROGRESS		WRITING PROGRESS		WRITING PROGRESS	

LOOKING AHEAD

Monthly Overview

How did my writing go this month?

Did I meet my writing and personal goals? Why or why not?

Am I happy with how I spent my time? If not, what changes will I make?

What did I learn this month that proved helpful?

What was my biggest time/ energy waster this month? How can I eliminate it?

What have I been procrastinating on?

FIND A PLACE TO SCHEDULE IT NEXT MONTH

What goals do I want to meet next month?

Month:

MONDAY	TUESDAY	WEDNESDAY

This Month's Focus

Social Media Goals

THURSDAY	FRIDAY	SATURDAY	SUNDAY

 Sales / Releases / Queries

Week Of

"Kindness is the language which the deaf can hear and the blind can see."
—Mark Twain

PRIORITY GOALS

TO DO

DREAM GOALS

	MONDAY		TUESDAY		WEDNESDAY
	INTENTIONS		INTENTIONS		INTENTIONS
6:00		6:00		6:00	
6:30		6:30		6:30	
7:00		7:00		7:00	
7:30		7:30		7:30	
8:00		8:00		8:00	
8:30		8:30		8:30	
9:00		9:00		9:00	
9:30		9:30		9:30	
10:00		10:00		10:00	
10:30		10:30		10:30	
11:00		11:00		11:00	
11:30		11:30		11:30	
	I AM CREATIVE		MY WORDS MATTER		LIFE IS GOOD
12:00		12:00		12:00	
12:30		12:30		12:30	
1:00		1:00		1:00	
1:30		1:30		1:30	
2:00		2:00		2:00	
2:30		2:30		2:30	
3:00		3:00		3:00	
3:30		3:30		3:30	
4:00		4:00		4:00	
4:30		4:30		4:30	
5:00		5:00		5:00	
5:30		5:30		5:30	
6:00		6:00		6:00	
6:30		6:30		6:30	
7:00		7:00		7:00	
7:30		7:30		7:30	
8:00		8:00		8:00	
WRITING PROGRESS		WRITING PROGRESS		WRITING PROGRESS	

GRATITUDES

THURSDAY		FRIDAY		SATURDAY		SUNDAY	
INTENTIONS		INTENTIONS		INTENTIONS		INTENTIONS	
6:00		6:00		6:00		6:00	
6:30		6:30		6:30		6:30	
7:00		7:00		7:00		7:00	
7:30		7:30		7:30		7:30	
8:00		8:00		8:00		8:00	
8:30		8:30		8:30		8:30	
9:00		9:00		9:00		9:00	
9:30		9:30		9:30		9:30	
10:00		10:00		10:00		10:00	
10:30		10:30		10:30		10:30	
11:00		11:00		11:00		11:00	
11:30		11:30		11:30		11:30	
	I MEET MY GOALS		BUILDING MY DREAMS		NO EXCUSES		I AM AN AUTHOR
12:00		12:00		12:00		12:00	
12:30		12:30		12:30		12:30	
1:00		1:00		1:00		1:00	
1:30		1:30		1:30		1:30	
2:00		2:00		2:00		2:00	
2:30		2:30		2:30		2:30	
3:00		3:00		3:00		3:00	
3:30		3:30		3:30		3:30	
4:00		4:00		4:00		4:00	
4:30		4:30		4:30		4:30	
5:00		5:00		5:00		5:00	
5:30		5:30		5:30		5:30	
6:00		6:00		6:00		6:00	
6:30		6:30		6:30		6:30	
7:00		7:00		7:00		7:00	
7:30		7:30		7:30		7:30	
8:00		8:00		8:00		8:00	
WRITING PROGRESS		WRITING PROGRESS		WRITING PROGRESS		WRITING PROGRESS	

LOOKING AHEAD

Week Of

"Powerful writing may make you vulnerable... but it gives your readers great strength."
—*Demi Stevens*

PRIORITY GOALS

TO DO

DREAM GOALS

	MONDAY		TUESDAY		WEDNESDAY
	INTENTIONS		INTENTIONS		INTENTIONS
6:00		6:00		6:00	
6:30		6:30		6:30	
7:00		7:00		7:00	
7:30		7:30		7:30	
8:00		8:00		8:00	
8:30		8:30		8:30	
9:00		9:00		9:00	
9:30		9:30		9:30	
10:00		10:00		10:00	
10:30		10:30		10:30	
11:00		11:00		11:00	
11:30		11:30		11:30	
	I AM CREATIVE		MY WORDS MATTER		LIFE IS GOOD
12:00		12:00		12:00	
12:30		12:30		12:30	
1:00		1:00		1:00	
1:30		1:30		1:30	
2:00		2:00		2:00	
2:30		2:30		2:30	
3:00		3:00		3:00	
3:30		3:30		3:30	
4:00		4:00		4:00	
4:30		4:30		4:30	
5:00		5:00		5:00	
5:30		5:30		5:30	
6:00		6:00		6:00	
6:30		6:30		6:30	
7:00		7:00		7:00	
7:30		7:30		7:30	
8:00		8:00		8:00	
WRITING PROGRESS		WRITING PROGRESS		WRITING PROGRESS	
GRATITUDES					

THURSDAY		FRIDAY		SATURDAY		SUNDAY	
INTENTIONS		INTENTIONS		INTENTIONS		INTENTIONS	
6:00		6:00		6:00		6:00	
6:30		6:30		6:30		6:30	
7:00		7:00		7:00		7:00	
7:30		7:30		7:30		7:30	
8:00		8:00		8:00		8:00	
8:30		8:30		8:30		8:30	
9:00		9:00		9:00		9:00	
9:30		9:30		9:30		9:30	
10:00		10:00		10:00		10:00	
10:30		10:30		10:30		10:30	
11:00		11:00		11:00		11:00	
11:30		11:30		11:30		11:30	
	I MEET MY GOALS		BUILDING MY DREAMS		NO EXCUSES		I AM AN AUTHOR
12:00		12:00		12:00		12:00	
12:30		12:30		12:30		12:30	
1:00		1:00		1:00		1:00	
1:30		1:30		1:30		1:30	
2:00		2:00		2:00		2:00	
2:30		2:30		2:30		2:30	
3:00		3:00		3:00		3:00	
3:30		3:30		3:30		3:30	
4:00		4:00		4:00		4:00	
4:30		4:30		4:30		4:30	
5:00		5:00		5:00		5:00	
5:30		5:30		5:30		5:30	
6:00		6:00		6:00		6:00	
6:30		6:30		6:30		6:30	
7:00		7:00		7:00		7:00	
7:30		7:30		7:30		7:30	
8:00		8:00		8:00		8:00	
WRITING PROGRESS		WRITING PROGRESS		WRITING PROGRESS		WRITING PROGRESS	

LOOKING AHEAD

Week Of

"Optimism is the faith that leads to achievement."
—Helen Keller

PRIORITY GOALS

TO DO

DREAM GOALS

	MONDAY		TUESDAY		WEDNESDAY	
	INTENTIONS		INTENTIONS		INTENTIONS	
6:00		6:00		6:00		
6:30		6:30		6:30		
7:00		7:00		7:00		
7:30		7:30		7:30		
8:00		8:00		8:00		
8:30		8:30		8:30		
9:00		9:00		9:00		
9:30		9:30		9:30		
10:00		10:00		10:00		
10:30		10:30		10:30		
11:00		11:00		11:00		
11:30		11:30		11:30		
	I AM CREATIVE		MY WORDS MATTER		LIFE IS GOOD	
12:00		12:00		12:00		
12:30		12:30		12:30		
1:00		1:00		1:00		
1:30		1:30		1:30		
2:00		2:00		2:00		
2:30		2:30		2:30		
3:00		3:00		3:00		
3:30		3:30		3:30		
4:00		4:00		4:00		
4:30		4:30		4:30		
5:00		5:00		5:00		
5:30		5:30		5:30		
6:00		6:00		6:00		
6:30		6:30		6:30		
7:00		7:00		7:00		
7:30		7:30		7:30		
8:00		8:00		8:00		
WRITING PROGRESS		WRITING PROGRESS		WRITING PROGRESS		
GRATITUDES						

THURSDAY		FRIDAY		SATURDAY		SUNDAY	
INTENTIONS		INTENTIONS		INTENTIONS		INTENTIONS	
6:00		6:00		6:00		6:00	
6:30		6:30		6:30		6:30	
7:00		7:00		7:00		7:00	
7:30		7:30		7:30		7:30	
8:00		8:00		8:00		8:00	
8:30		8:30		8:30		8:30	
9:00		9:00		9:00		9:00	
9:30		9:30		9:30		9:30	
10:00		10:00		10:00		10:00	
10:30		10:30		10:30		10:30	
11:00		11:00		11:00		11:00	
11:30		11:30		11:30		11:30	
	I MEET MY GOALS		BUILDING MY DREAMS		NO EXCUSES		I AM AN AUTHOR
12:00		12:00		12:00		12:00	
12:30		12:30		12:30		12:30	
1:00		1:00		1:00		1:00	
1:30		1:30		1:30		1:30	
2:00		2:00		2:00		2:00	
2:30		2:30		2:30		2:30	
3:00		3:00		3:00		3:00	
3:30		3:30		3:30		3:30	
4:00		4:00		4:00		4:00	
4:30		4:30		4:30		4:30	
5:00		5:00		5:00		5:00	
5:30		5:30		5:30		5:30	
6:00		6:00		6:00		6:00	
6:30		6:30		6:30		6:30	
7:00		7:00		7:00		7:00	
7:30		7:30		7:30		7:30	
8:00		8:00		8:00		8:00	
WRITING PROGRESS		WRITING PROGRESS		WRITING PROGRESS		WRITING PROGRESS	

LOOKING AHEAD

Week Of

You're already good enough.

PRIORITY GOALS

TO DO

DREAM GOALS

	MONDAY		TUESDAY		WEDNESDAY
	INTENTIONS		INTENTIONS		INTENTIONS
6:00		6:00		6:00	
6:30		6:30		6:30	
7:00		7:00		7:00	
7:30		7:30		7:30	
8:00		8:00		8:00	
8:30		8:30		8:30	
9:00		9:00		9:00	
9:30		9:30		9:30	
10:00		10:00		10:00	
10:30		10:30		10:30	
11:00		11:00		11:00	
11:30		11:30		11:30	
	I AM CREATIVE		MY WORDS MATTER		LIFE IS GOOD
12:00		12:00		12:00	
12:30		12:30		12:30	
1:00		1:00		1:00	
1:30		1:30		1:30	
2:00		2:00		2:00	
2:30		2:30		2:30	
3:00		3:00		3:00	
3:30		3:30		3:30	
4:00		4:00		4:00	
4:30		4:30		4:30	
5:00		5:00		5:00	
5:30		5:30		5:30	
6:00		6:00		6:00	
6:30		6:30		6:30	
7:00		7:00		7:00	
7:30		7:30		7:30	
8:00		8:00		8:00	
WRITING PROGRESS		WRITING PROGRESS		WRITING PROGRESS	
GRATITUDES					

THURSDAY		FRIDAY		SATURDAY		SUNDAY	
INTENTIONS		INTENTIONS		INTENTIONS		INTENTIONS	
6:00		6:00		6:00		6:00	
6:30		6:30		6:30		6:30	
7:00		7:00		7:00		7:00	
7:30		7:30		7:30		7:30	
8:00		8:00		8:00		8:00	
8:30		8:30		8:30		8:30	
9:00		9:00		9:00		9:00	
9:30		9:30		9:30		9:30	
10:00		10:00		10:00		10:00	
10:30		10:30		10:30		10:30	
11:00		11:00		11:00		11:00	
11:30		11:30		11:30		11:30	
	I MEET MY GOALS		BUILDING MY DREAMS		NO EXCUSES		I AM AN AUTHOR
12:00		12:00		12:00		12:00	
12:30		12:30		12:30		12:30	
1:00		1:00		1:00		1:00	
1:30		1:30		1:30		1:30	
2:00		2:00		2:00		2:00	
2:30		2:30		2:30		2:30	
3:00		3:00		3:00		3:00	
3:30		3:30		3:30		3:30	
4:00		4:00		4:00		4:00	
4:30		4:30		4:30		4:30	
5:00		5:00		5:00		5:00	
5:30		5:30		5:30		5:30	
6:00		6:00		6:00		6:00	
6:30		6:30		6:30		6:30	
7:00		7:00		7:00		7:00	
7:30		7:30		7:30		7:30	
8:00		8:00		8:00		8:00	
WRITING PROGRESS		WRITING PROGRESS		WRITING PROGRESS		WRITING PROGRESS	

LOOKING AHEAD

Week Of

"Do a little more each day than you think you possibly can."
—Lowell Thomas

PRIORITY GOALS

TO DO

DREAM GOALS

	MONDAY		TUESDAY		WEDNESDAY
	INTENTIONS		INTENTIONS		INTENTIONS
6:00		6:00		6:00	
6:30		6:30		6:30	
7:00		7:00		7:00	
7:30		7:30		7:30	
8:00		8:00		8:00	
8:30		8:30		8:30	
9:00		9:00		9:00	
9:30		9:30		9:30	
10:00		10:00		10:00	
10:30		10:30		10:30	
11:00		11:00		11:00	
11:30		11:30		11:30	
	I AM CREATIVE		MY WORDS MATTER		LIFE IS GOOD
12:00		12:00		12:00	
12:30		12:30		12:30	
1:00		1:00		1:00	
1:30		1:30		1:30	
2:00		2:00		2:00	
2:30		2:30		2:30	
3:00		3:00		3:00	
3:30		3:30		3:30	
4:00		4:00		4:00	
4:30		4:30		4:30	
5:00		5:00		5:00	
5:30		5:30		5:30	
6:00		6:00		6:00	
6:30		6:30		6:30	
7:00		7:00		7:00	
7:30		7:30		7:30	
8:00		8:00		8:00	
WRITING PROGRESS		WRITING PROGRESS		WRITING PROGRESS	

GRATITUDES

THURSDAY		FRIDAY		SATURDAY		SUNDAY	
INTENTIONS		INTENTIONS		INTENTIONS		INTENTIONS	
6:00		6:00		6:00		6:00	
6:30		6:30		6:30		6:30	
7:00		7:00		7:00		7:00	
7:30		7:30		7:30		7:30	
8:00		8:00		8:00		8:00	
8:30		8:30		8:30		8:30	
9:00		9:00		9:00		9:00	
9:30		9:30		9:30		9:30	
10:00		10:00		10:00		10:00	
10:30		10:30		10:30		10:30	
11:00		11:00		11:00		11:00	
11:30		11:30		11:30		11:30	
	I MEET MY GOALS		BUILDING MY DREAMS		NO EXCUSES		I AM AN AUTHOR
12:00		12:00		12:00		12:00	
12:30		12:30		12:30		12:30	
1:00		1:00		1:00		1:00	
1:30		1:30		1:30		1:30	
2:00		2:00		2:00		2:00	
2:30		2:30		2:30		2:30	
3:00		3:00		3:00		3:00	
3:30		3:30		3:30		3:30	
4:00		4:00		4:00		4:00	
4:30		4:30		4:30		4:30	
5:00		5:00		5:00		5:00	
5:30		5:30		5:30		5:30	
6:00		6:00		6:00		6:00	
6:30		6:30		6:30		6:30	
7:00		7:00		7:00		7:00	
7:30		7:30		7:30		7:30	
8:00		8:00		8:00		8:00	
WRITING PROGRESS		WRITING PROGRESS		WRITING PROGRESS		WRITING PROGRESS	

LOOKING AHEAD

Quarterly Overview

**Am I still on target with my yearly goals?
Or have I chosen a new path?**

What interfered with my progress?

What can I do next quarter to eliminate these obstacles?

What do I need to let go of this coming quarter?

What happened this quarter that I need to reframe positively?

How do my work and activities reflect the yearly word I chose?

What do I hope to accomplish next quarter?

Month:

MONDAY	TUESDAY	WEDNESDAY

This Month's Focus

Social Media Goals

THURSDAY	FRIDAY	SATURDAY	SUNDAY

Sales / Releases / Queries

Week Of

"We write by the light of every story we have ever read."
—Richard Peck

PRIORITY GOALS

TO DO

DREAM GOALS

	MONDAY		TUESDAY		WEDNESDAY
	INTENTIONS		INTENTIONS		INTENTIONS
6:00		6:00		6:00	
6:30		6:30		6:30	
7:00		7:00		7:00	
7:30		7:30		7:30	
8:00		8:00		8:00	
8:30		8:30		8:30	
9:00		9:00		9:00	
9:30		9:30		9:30	
10:00		10:00		10:00	
10:30		10:30		10:30	
11:00		11:00		11:00	
11:30		11:30		11:30	
	I AM CREATIVE		MY WORDS MATTER		LIFE IS GOOD
12:00		12:00		12:00	
12:30		12:30		12:30	
1:00		1:00		1:00	
1:30		1:30		1:30	
2:00		2:00		2:00	
2:30		2:30		2:30	
3:00		3:00		3:00	
3:30		3:30		3:30	
4:00		4:00		4:00	
4:30		4:30		4:30	
5:00		5:00		5:00	
5:30		5:30		5:30	
6:00		6:00		6:00	
6:30		6:30		6:30	
7:00		7:00		7:00	
7:30		7:30		7:30	
8:00		8:00		8:00	
WRITING PROGRESS		WRITING PROGRESS		WRITING PROGRESS	
GRATITUDES					

THURSDAY		FRIDAY		SATURDAY		SUNDAY	
INTENTIONS		INTENTIONS		INTENTIONS		INTENTIONS	
6:00		6:00		6:00		6:00	
6:30		6:30		6:30		6:30	
7:00		7:00		7:00		7:00	
7:30		7:30		7:30		7:30	
8:00		8:00		8:00		8:00	
8:30		8:30		8:30		8:30	
9:00		9:00		9:00		9:00	
9:30		9:30		9:30		9:30	
10:00		10:00		10:00		10:00	
10:30		10:30		10:30		10:30	
11:00		11:00		11:00		11:00	
11:30		11:30		11:30		11:30	
	I MEET MY GOALS		BUILDING MY DREAMS		NO EXCUSES		I AM AN AUTHOR
12:00		12:00		12:00		12:00	
12:30		12:30		12:30		12:30	
1:00		1:00		1:00		1:00	
1:30		1:30		1:30		1:30	
2:00		2:00		2:00		2:00	
2:30		2:30		2:30		2:30	
3:00		3:00		3:00		3:00	
3:30		3:30		3:30		3:30	
4:00		4:00		4:00		4:00	
4:30		4:30		4:30		4:30	
5:00		5:00		5:00		5:00	
5:30		5:30		5:30		5:30	
6:00		6:00		6:00		6:00	
6:30		6:30		6:30		6:30	
7:00		7:00		7:00		7:00	
7:30		7:30		7:30		7:30	
8:00		8:00		8:00		8:00	
WRITING PROGRESS		WRITING PROGRESS		WRITING PROGRESS		WRITING PROGRESS	

LOOKING AHEAD

Week Of

Create the life you've always wanted.

PRIORITY GOALS

TO DO

DREAM GOALS

	MONDAY INTENTIONS		TUESDAY INTENTIONS		WEDNESDAY INTENTIONS	
6:00		6:00		6:00		
6:30		6:30		6:30		
7:00		7:00		7:00		
7:30		7:30		7:30		
8:00		8:00		8:00		
8:30		8:30		8:30		
9:00		9:00		9:00		
9:30		9:30		9:30		
10:00		10:00		10:00		
10:30		10:30		10:30		
11:00		11:00		11:00		
11:30		11:30		11:30		
	I AM CREATIVE		MY WORDS MATTER		LIFE IS GOOD	
12:00		12:00		12:00		
12:30		12:30		12:30		
1:00		1:00		1:00		
1:30		1:30		1:30		
2:00		2:00		2:00		
2:30		2:30		2:30		
3:00		3:00		3:00		
3:30		3:30		3:30		
4:00		4:00		4:00		
4:30		4:30		4:30		
5:00		5:00		5:00		
5:30		5:30		5:30		
6:00		6:00		6:00		
6:30		6:30		6:30		
7:00		7:00		7:00		
7:30		7:30		7:30		
8:00		8:00		8:00		
WRITING PROGRESS		WRITING PROGRESS		WRITING PROGRESS		
GRATITUDES						

THURSDAY		FRIDAY		SATURDAY		SUNDAY	
INTENTIONS		INTENTIONS		INTENTIONS		INTENTIONS	
6:00		6:00		6:00		6:00	
6:30		6:30		6:30		6:30	
7:00		7:00		7:00		7:00	
7:30		7:30		7:30		7:30	
8:00		8:00		8:00		8:00	
8:30		8:30		8:30		8:30	
9:00		9:00		9:00		9:00	
9:30		9:30		9:30		9:30	
10:00		10:00		10:00		10:00	
10:30		10:30		10:30		10:30	
11:00		11:00		11:00		11:00	
11:30		11:30		11:30		11:30	
	I MEET MY GOALS		BUILDING MY DREAMS		NO EXCUSES		I AM AN AUTHOR
12:00		12:00		12:00		12:00	
12:30		12:30		12:30		12:30	
1:00		1:00		1:00		1:00	
1:30		1:30		1:30		1:30	
2:00		2:00		2:00		2:00	
2:30		2:30		2:30		2:30	
3:00		3:00		3:00		3:00	
3:30		3:30		3:30		3:30	
4:00		4:00		4:00		4:00	
4:30		4:30		4:30		4:30	
5:00		5:00		5:00		5:00	
5:30		5:30		5:30		5:30	
6:00		6:00		6:00		6:00	
6:30		6:30		6:30		6:30	
7:00		7:00		7:00		7:00	
7:30		7:30		7:30		7:30	
8:00		8:00		8:00		8:00	
WRITING PROGRESS		WRITING PROGRESS		WRITING PROGRESS		WRITING PROGRESS	

LOOKING AHEAD

Week Of

"I open to all the beautiful possibilities blossoming before me."
—Leonie Dawson

PRIORITY GOALS

TO DO

DREAM GOALS

	MONDAY		TUESDAY		WEDNESDAY
	INTENTIONS		INTENTIONS		INTENTIONS
6:00		6:00		6:00	
6:30		6:30		6:30	
7:00		7:00		7:00	
7:30		7:30		7:30	
8:00		8:00		8:00	
8:30		8:30		8:30	
9:00		9:00		9:00	
9:30		9:30		9:30	
10:00		10:00		10:00	
10:30		10:30		10:30	
11:00		11:00		11:00	
11:30		11:30		11:30	
	I AM CREATIVE		MY WORDS MATTER		LIFE IS GOOD
12:00		12:00		12:00	
12:30		12:30		12:30	
1:00		1:00		1:00	
1:30		1:30		1:30	
2:00		2:00		2:00	
2:30		2:30		2:30	
3:00		3:00		3:00	
3:30		3:30		3:30	
4:00		4:00		4:00	
4:30		4:30		4:30	
5:00		5:00		5:00	
5:30		5:30		5:30	
6:00		6:00		6:00	
6:30		6:30		6:30	
7:00		7:00		7:00	
7:30		7:30		7:30	
8:00		8:00		8:00	
WRITING PROGRESS		WRITING PROGRESS		WRITING PROGRESS	
GRATITUDES					

THURSDAY		FRIDAY		SATURDAY		SUNDAY	
INTENTIONS		INTENTIONS		INTENTIONS		INTENTIONS	
6:00		6:00		6:00		6:00	
6:30		6:30		6:30		6:30	
7:00		7:00		7:00		7:00	
7:30		7:30		7:30		7:30	
8:00		8:00		8:00		8:00	
8:30		8:30		8:30		8:30	
9:00		9:00		9:00		9:00	
9:30		9:30		9:30		9:30	
10:00		10:00		10:00		10:00	
10:30		10:30		10:30		10:30	
11:00		11:00		11:00		11:00	
11:30		11:30		11:30		11:30	
	I MEET MY GOALS		BUILDING MY DREAMS		NO EXCUSES		I AM AN AUTHOR
12:00		12:00		12:00		12:00	
12:30		12:30		12:30		12:30	
1:00		1:00		1:00		1:00	
1:30		1:30		1:30		1:30	
2:00		2:00		2:00		2:00	
2:30		2:30		2:30		2:30	
3:00		3:00		3:00		3:00	
3:30		3:30		3:30		3:30	
4:00		4:00		4:00		4:00	
4:30		4:30		4:30		4:30	
5:00		5:00		5:00		5:00	
5:30		5:30		5:30		5:30	
6:00		6:00		6:00		6:00	
6:30		6:30		6:30		6:30	
7:00		7:00		7:00		7:00	
7:30		7:30		7:30		7:30	
8:00		8:00		8:00		8:00	
WRITING PROGRESS		WRITING PROGRESS		WRITING PROGRESS		WRITING PROGRESS	

LOOKING AHEAD

Week Of

Tomorrow is a new day... but why wait?

PRIORITY GOALS

TO DO

DREAM GOALS

	MONDAY		TUESDAY		WEDNESDAY
	INTENTIONS		INTENTIONS		INTENTIONS
6:00		6:00		6:00	
6:30		6:30		6:30	
7:00		7:00		7:00	
7:30		7:30		7:30	
8:00		8:00		8:00	
8:30		8:30		8:30	
9:00		9:00		9:00	
9:30		9:30		9:30	
10:00		10:00		10:00	
10:30		10:30		10:30	
11:00		11:00		11:00	
11:30		11:30		11:30	
	I AM CREATIVE		MY WORDS MATTER		LIFE IS GOOD
12:00		12:00		12:00	
12:30		12:30		12:30	
1:00		1:00		1:00	
1:30		1:30		1:30	
2:00		2:00		2:00	
2:30		2:30		2:30	
3:00		3:00		3:00	
3:30		3:30		3:30	
4:00		4:00		4:00	
4:30		4:30		4:30	
5:00		5:00		5:00	
5:30		5:30		5:30	
6:00		6:00		6:00	
6:30		6:30		6:30	
7:00		7:00		7:00	
7:30		7:30		7:30	
8:00		8:00		8:00	
WRITING PROGRESS		WRITING PROGRESS		WRITING PROGRESS	
GRATITUDES					

THURSDAY		FRIDAY		SATURDAY		SUNDAY	
INTENTIONS		INTENTIONS		INTENTIONS		INTENTIONS	
6:00		6:00		6:00		6:00	
6:30		6:30		6:30		6:30	
7:00		7:00		7:00		7:00	
7:30		7:30		7:30		7:30	
8:00		8:00		8:00		8:00	
8:30		8:30		8:30		8:30	
9:00		9:00		9:00		9:00	
9:30		9:30		9:30		9:30	
10:00		10:00		10:00		10:00	
10:30		10:30		10:30		10:30	
11:00		11:00		11:00		11:00	
11:30		11:30		11:30		11:30	
	I MEET MY GOALS		BUILDING MY DREAMS		NO EXCUSES		I AM AN AUTHOR
12:00		12:00		12:00		12:00	
12:30		12:30		12:30		12:30	
1:00		1:00		1:00		1:00	
1:30		1:30		1:30		1:30	
2:00		2:00		2:00		2:00	
2:30		2:30		2:30		2:30	
3:00		3:00		3:00		3:00	
3:30		3:30		3:30		3:30	
4:00		4:00		4:00		4:00	
4:30		4:30		4:30		4:30	
5:00		5:00		5:00		5:00	
5:30		5:30		5:30		5:30	
6:00		6:00		6:00		6:00	
6:30		6:30		6:30		6:30	
7:00		7:00		7:00		7:00	
7:30		7:30		7:30		7:30	
8:00		8:00		8:00		8:00	
WRITING PROGRESS		WRITING PROGRESS		WRITING PROGRESS		WRITING PROGRESS	

LOOKING AHEAD

Monthly Overview

How did my writing go this month?

Did I meet my writing and personal goals? Why or why not?

Am I happy with how I spent my time? If not, what changes will I make?

What did I learn this month that proved helpful?

What was my biggest time/ energy waster this month? How can I eliminate it?

What have I been procrastinating on?

FIND A PLACE TO SCHEDULE IT NEXT MONTH

What goals do I want to meet next month?

Month:

MONDAY	TUESDAY	WEDNESDAY

This Month's Focus

Social Media Goals

THURSDAY	FRIDAY	SATURDAY	SUNDAY

 Sales / Releases / Queries

Week Of

"Your writing doesn't have to be perfect, you only have to start."

PRIORITY GOALS

TO DO

DREAM GOALS

	MONDAY		TUESDAY		WEDNESDAY	
	INTENTIONS		INTENTIONS		INTENTIONS	
6:00		6:00		6:00		
6:30		6:30		6:30		
7:00		7:00		7:00		
7:30		7:30		7:30		
8:00		8:00		8:00		
8:30		8:30		8:30		
9:00		9:00		9:00		
9:30		9:30		9:30		
10:00		10:00		10:00		
10:30		10:30		10:30		
11:00		11:00		11:00		
11:30		11:30		11:30		
	I AM CREATIVE		MY WORDS MATTER		LIFE IS GOOD	
12:00		12:00		12:00		
12:30		12:30		12:30		
1:00		1:00		1:00		
1:30		1:30		1:30		
2:00		2:00		2:00		
2:30		2:30		2:30		
3:00		3:00		3:00		
3:30		3:30		3:30		
4:00		4:00		4:00		
4:30		4:30		4:30		
5:00		5:00		5:00		
5:30		5:30		5:30		
6:00		6:00		6:00		
6:30		6:30		6:30		
7:00		7:00		7:00		
7:30		7:30		7:30		
8:00		8:00		8:00		
WRITING PROGRESS		WRITING PROGRESS		WRITING PROGRESS		

GRATITUDES

THURSDAY		FRIDAY		SATURDAY		SUNDAY	
INTENTIONS		INTENTIONS		INTENTIONS		INTENTIONS	
6:00		6:00		6:00		6:00	
6:30		6:30		6:30		6:30	
7:00		7:00		7:00		7:00	
7:30		7:30		7:30		7:30	
8:00		8:00		8:00		8:00	
8:30		8:30		8:30		8:30	
9:00		9:00		9:00		9:00	
9:30		9:30		9:30		9:30	
10:00		10:00		10:00		10:00	
10:30		10:30		10:30		10:30	
11:00		11:00		11:00		11:00	
11:30		11:30		11:30		11:30	
	I MEET MY GOALS		BUILDING MY DREAMS		NO EXCUSES		I AM AN AUTHOR
12:00		12:00		12:00		12:00	
12:30		12:30		12:30		12:30	
1:00		1:00		1:00		1:00	
1:30		1:30		1:30		1:30	
2:00		2:00		2:00		2:00	
2:30		2:30		2:30		2:30	
3:00		3:00		3:00		3:00	
3:30		3:30		3:30		3:30	
4:00		4:00		4:00		4:00	
4:30		4:30		4:30		4:30	
5:00		5:00		5:00		5:00	
5:30		5:30		5:30		5:30	
6:00		6:00		6:00		6:00	
6:30		6:30		6:30		6:30	
7:00		7:00		7:00		7:00	
7:30		7:30		7:30		7:30	
8:00		8:00		8:00		8:00	
WRITING PROGRESS		WRITING PROGRESS		WRITING PROGRESS		WRITING PROGRESS	

LOOKING AHEAD

Week Of

"PLOT is a 4-letter word."
—Demi Stevens

PRIORITY GOALS

TO DO

DREAM GOALS

	MONDAY		TUESDAY		WEDNESDAY
	INTENTIONS		INTENTIONS		INTENTIONS
6:00		6:00		6:00	
6:30		6:30		6:30	
7:00		7:00		7:00	
7:30		7:30		7:30	
8:00		8:00		8:00	
8:30		8:30		8:30	
9:00		9:00		9:00	
9:30		9:30		9:30	
10:00		10:00		10:00	
10:30		10:30		10:30	
11:00		11:00		11:00	
11:30		11:30		11:30	
	I AM CREATIVE		MY WORDS MATTER		LIFE IS GOOD
12:00		12:00		12:00	
12:30		12:30		12:30	
1:00		1:00		1:00	
1:30		1:30		1:30	
2:00		2:00		2:00	
2:30		2:30		2:30	
3:00		3:00		3:00	
3:30		3:30		3:30	
4:00		4:00		4:00	
4:30		4:30		4:30	
5:00		5:00		5:00	
5:30		5:30		5:30	
6:00		6:00		6:00	
6:30		6:30		6:30	
7:00		7:00		7:00	
7:30		7:30		7:30	
8:00		8:00		8:00	
WRITING PROGRESS		WRITING PROGRESS		WRITING PROGRESS	
GRATITUDES					

THURSDAY		FRIDAY		SATURDAY		SUNDAY	
INTENTIONS		INTENTIONS		INTENTIONS		INTENTIONS	
6:00		6:00		6:00		6:00	
6:30		6:30		6:30		6:30	
7:00		7:00		7:00		7:00	
7:30		7:30		7:30		7:30	
8:00		8:00		8:00		8:00	
8:30		8:30		8:30		8:30	
9:00		9:00		9:00		9:00	
9:30		9:30		9:30		9:30	
10:00		10:00		10:00		10:00	
10:30		10:30		10:30		10:30	
11:00		11:00		11:00		11:00	
11:30		11:30		11:30		11:30	
	I MEET MY GOALS		BUILDING MY DREAMS		NO EXCUSES		I AM AN AUTHOR
12:00		12:00		12:00		12:00	
12:30		12:30		12:30		12:30	
1:00		1:00		1:00		1:00	
1:30		1:30		1:30		1:30	
2:00		2:00		2:00		2:00	
2:30		2:30		2:30		2:30	
3:00		3:00		3:00		3:00	
3:30		3:30		3:30		3:30	
4:00		4:00		4:00		4:00	
4:30		4:30		4:30		4:30	
5:00		5:00		5:00		5:00	
5:30		5:30		5:30		5:30	
6:00		6:00		6:00		6:00	
6:30		6:30		6:30		6:30	
7:00		7:00		7:00		7:00	
7:30		7:30		7:30		7:30	
8:00		8:00		8:00		8:00	
WRITING PROGRESS		WRITING PROGRESS		WRITING PROGRESS		WRITING PROGRESS	

LOOKING AHEAD

Week Of

*"Never give up,
for that is just the
place
and time that
the tide will turn."*
—Harriet Beecher
Stowe

PRIORITY GOALS

TO DO

DREAM GOALS

	MONDAY		TUESDAY		WEDNESDAY
	INTENTIONS		INTENTIONS		INTENTIONS
6:00		6:00		6:00	
6:30		6:30		6:30	
7:00		7:00		7:00	
7:30		7:30		7:30	
8:00		8:00		8:00	
8:30		8:30		8:30	
9:00		9:00		9:00	
9:30		9:30		9:30	
10:00		10:00		10:00	
10:30		10:30		10:30	
11:00		11:00		11:00	
11:30		11:30		11:30	
	I AM CREATIVE		MY WORDS MATTER		LIFE IS GOOD
12:00		12:00		12:00	
12:30		12:30		12:30	
1:00		1:00		1:00	
1:30		1:30		1:30	
2:00		2:00		2:00	
2:30		2:30		2:30	
3:00		3:00		3:00	
3:30		3:30		3:30	
4:00		4:00		4:00	
4:30		4:30		4:30	
5:00		5:00		5:00	
5:30		5:30		5:30	
6:00		6:00		6:00	
6:30		6:30		6:30	
7:00		7:00		7:00	
7:30		7:30		7:30	
8:00		8:00		8:00	
WRITING PROGRESS		WRITING PROGRESS		WRITING PROGRESS	
GRATITUDES					

THURSDAY		FRIDAY		SATURDAY		SUNDAY	
INTENTIONS		INTENTIONS		INTENTIONS		INTENTIONS	
6:00		6:00		6:00		6:00	
6:30		6:30		6:30		6:30	
7:00		7:00		7:00		7:00	
7:30		7:30		7:30		7:30	
8:00		8:00		8:00		8:00	
8:30		8:30		8:30		8:30	
9:00		9:00		9:00		9:00	
9:30		9:30		9:30		9:30	
10:00		10:00		10:00		10:00	
10:30		10:30		10:30		10:30	
11:00		11:00		11:00		11:00	
11:30		11:30		11:30		11:30	
	I MEET MY GOALS		BUILDING MY DREAMS		NO EXCUSES		I AM AN AUTHOR
12:00		12:00		12:00		12:00	
12:30		12:30		12:30		12:30	
1:00		1:00		1:00		1:00	
1:30		1:30		1:30		1:30	
2:00		2:00		2:00		2:00	
2:30		2:30		2:30		2:30	
3:00		3:00		3:00		3:00	
3:30		3:30		3:30		3:30	
4:00		4:00		4:00		4:00	
4:30		4:30		4:30		4:30	
5:00		5:00		5:00		5:00	
5:30		5:30		5:30		5:30	
6:00		6:00		6:00		6:00	
6:30		6:30		6:30		6:30	
7:00		7:00		7:00		7:00	
7:30		7:30		7:30		7:30	
8:00		8:00		8:00		8:00	
WRITING PROGRESS		WRITING PROGRESS		WRITING PROGRESS		WRITING PROGRESS	

LOOKING AHEAD

Week Of

*"I love deadlines.
I like the
whooshing sound
they make
as they fly by."*
—Douglas Adams

PRIORITY GOALS

TO DO

DREAM GOALS

	MONDAY		TUESDAY		WEDNESDAY
	INTENTIONS		INTENTIONS		INTENTIONS
6:00		6:00		6:00	
6:30		6:30		6:30	
7:00		7:00		7:00	
7:30		7:30		7:30	
8:00		8:00		8:00	
8:30		8:30		8:30	
9:00		9:00		9:00	
9:30		9:30		9:30	
10:00		10:00		10:00	
10:30		10:30		10:30	
11:00		11:00		11:00	
11:30		11:30		11:30	
	I AM CREATIVE		MY WORDS MATTER		LIFE IS GOOD
12:00		12:00		12:00	
12:30		12:30		12:30	
1:00		1:00		1:00	
1:30		1:30		1:30	
2:00		2:00		2:00	
2:30		2:30		2:30	
3:00		3:00		3:00	
3:30		3:30		3:30	
4:00		4:00		4:00	
4:30		4:30		4:30	
5:00		5:00		5:00	
5:30		5:30		5:30	
6:00		6:00		6:00	
6:30		6:30		6:30	
7:00		7:00		7:00	
7:30		7:30		7:30	
8:00		8:00		8:00	
WRITING PROGRESS		WRITING PROGRESS		WRITING PROGRESS	
GRATITUDES					

THURSDAY		FRIDAY		SATURDAY		SUNDAY	
INTENTIONS		INTENTIONS		INTENTIONS		INTENTIONS	
6:00		6:00		6:00		6:00	
6:30		6:30		6:30		6:30	
7:00		7:00		7:00		7:00	
7:30		7:30		7:30		7:30	
8:00		8:00		8:00		8:00	
8:30		8:30		8:30		8:30	
9:00		9:00		9:00		9:00	
9:30		9:30		9:30		9:30	
10:00		10:00		10:00		10:00	
10:30		10:30		10:30		10:30	
11:00		11:00		11:00		11:00	
11:30		11:30		11:30		11:30	
	I MEET MY GOALS		BUILDING MY DREAMS		NO EXCUSES		I AM AN AUTHOR
12:00		12:00		12:00		12:00	
12:30		12:30		12:30		12:30	
1:00		1:00		1:00		1:00	
1:30		1:30		1:30		1:30	
2:00		2:00		2:00		2:00	
2:30		2:30		2:30		2:30	
3:00		3:00		3:00		3:00	
3:30		3:30		3:30		3:30	
4:00		4:00		4:00		4:00	
4:30		4:30		4:30		4:30	
5:00		5:00		5:00		5:00	
5:30		5:30		5:30		5:30	
6:00		6:00		6:00		6:00	
6:30		6:30		6:30		6:30	
7:00		7:00		7:00		7:00	
7:30		7:30		7:30		7:30	
8:00		8:00		8:00		8:00	
WRITING PROGRESS		WRITING PROGRESS		WRITING PROGRESS		WRITING PROGRESS	

LOOKING AHEAD

TIME TO ORDER YOUR NEW PLANNER! Visit yotbpress.com/authorjourney

Monthly Overview

How did my writing go this month?

Did I meet my writing and personal goals? Why or why not?

Am I happy with how I spent my time?
If not, what changes will I make?

What did I learn this month that proved helpful?

What was my biggest time/ energy waster this month? How can I eliminate it?

What have I been procrastinating on?

FIND A PLACE TO SCHEDULE IT NEXT MONTH

What goals do I want to meet next month?

Month:

MONDAY	TUESDAY	WEDNESDAY

This Month's Focus

Social Media Goals

THURSDAY	FRIDAY	SATURDAY	SUNDAY

 Sales / Releases / Queries

Week Of

"No one's going to find your work until you put it in front of them."
—Demi Stevens

PRIORITY GOALS

TO DO

DREAM GOALS

	MONDAY		TUESDAY		WEDNESDAY
	INTENTIONS		INTENTIONS		INTENTIONS
6:00		6:00		6:00	
6:30		6:30		6:30	
7:00		7:00		7:00	
7:30		7:30		7:30	
8:00		8:00		8:00	
8:30		8:30		8:30	
9:00		9:00		9:00	
9:30		9:30		9:30	
10:00		10:00		10:00	
10:30		10:30		10:30	
11:00		11:00		11:00	
11:30		11:30		11:30	
	I AM CREATIVE		MY WORDS MATTER		LIFE IS GOOD
12:00		12:00		12:00	
12:30		12:30		12:30	
1:00		1:00		1:00	
1:30		1:30		1:30	
2:00		2:00		2:00	
2:30		2:30		2:30	
3:00		3:00		3:00	
3:30		3:30		3:30	
4:00		4:00		4:00	
4:30		4:30		4:30	
5:00		5:00		5:00	
5:30		5:30		5:30	
6:00		6:00		6:00	
6:30		6:30		6:30	
7:00		7:00		7:00	
7:30		7:30		7:30	
8:00		8:00		8:00	
WRITING PROGRESS		WRITING PROGRESS		WRITING PROGRESS	

GRATITUDES

THURSDAY		FRIDAY		SATURDAY		SUNDAY	
INTENTIONS		INTENTIONS		INTENTIONS		INTENTIONS	
6:00		6:00		6:00		6:00	
6:30		6:30		6:30		6:30	
7:00		7:00		7:00		7:00	
7:30		7:30		7:30		7:30	
8:00		8:00		8:00		8:00	
8:30		8:30		8:30		8:30	
9:00		9:00		9:00		9:00	
9:30		9:30		9:30		9:30	
10:00		10:00		10:00		10:00	
10:30		10:30		10:30		10:30	
11:00		11:00		11:00		11:00	
11:30		11:30		11:30		11:30	
	I MEET MY GOALS		BUILDING MY DREAMS		NO EXCUSES		I AM AN AUTHOR
12:00		12:00		12:00		12:00	
12:30		12:30		12:30		12:30	
1:00		1:00		1:00		1:00	
1:30		1:30		1:30		1:30	
2:00		2:00		2:00		2:00	
2:30		2:30		2:30		2:30	
3:00		3:00		3:00		3:00	
3:30		3:30		3:30		3:30	
4:00		4:00		4:00		4:00	
4:30		4:30		4:30		4:30	
5:00		5:00		5:00		5:00	
5:30		5:30		5:30		5:30	
6:00		6:00		6:00		6:00	
6:30		6:30		6:30		6:30	
7:00		7:00		7:00		7:00	
7:30		7:30		7:30		7:30	
8:00		8:00		8:00		8:00	
WRITING PROGRESS		WRITING PROGRESS		WRITING PROGRESS		WRITING PROGRESS	

LOOKING AHEAD

Week Of

"Be kind whenever possible. It is always possible."
—Dalai Lama

PRIORITY GOALS

TO DO

DREAM GOALS

	MONDAY		TUESDAY		WEDNESDAY
	INTENTIONS		INTENTIONS		INTENTIONS
6:00		6:00		6:00	
6:30		6:30		6:30	
7:00		7:00		7:00	
7:30		7:30		7:30	
8:00		8:00		8:00	
8:30		8:30		8:30	
9:00		9:00		9:00	
9:30		9:30		9:30	
10:00		10:00		10:00	
10:30		10:30		10:30	
11:00		11:00		11:00	
11:30		11:30		11:30	
	I AM CREATIVE		MY WORDS MATTER		LIFE IS GOOD
12:00		12:00		12:00	
12:30		12:30		12:30	
1:00		1:00		1:00	
1:30		1:30		1:30	
2:00		2:00		2:00	
2:30		2:30		2:30	
3:00		3:00		3:00	
3:30		3:30		3:30	
4:00		4:00		4:00	
4:30		4:30		4:30	
5:00		5:00		5:00	
5:30		5:30		5:30	
6:00		6:00		6:00	
6:30		6:30		6:30	
7:00		7:00		7:00	
7:30		7:30		7:30	
8:00		8:00		8:00	
WRITING PROGRESS		WRITING PROGRESS		WRITING PROGRESS	
GRATITUDES					

THURSDAY		FRIDAY		SATURDAY		SUNDAY	
INTENTIONS		INTENTIONS		INTENTIONS		INTENTIONS	
6:00		6:00		6:00		6:00	
6:30		6:30		6:30		6:30	
7:00		7:00		7:00		7:00	
7:30		7:30		7:30		7:30	
8:00		8:00		8:00		8:00	
8:30		8:30		8:30		8:30	
9:00		9:00		9:00		9:00	
9:30		9:30		9:30		9:30	
10:00		10:00		10:00		10:00	
10:30		10:30		10:30		10:30	
11:00		11:00		11:00		11:00	
11:30		11:30		11:30		11:30	
	I MEET MY GOALS		BUILDING MY DREAMS		NO EXCUSES		I AM AN AUTHOR
12:00		12:00		12:00		12:00	
12:30		12:30		12:30		12:30	
1:00		1:00		1:00		1:00	
1:30		1:30		1:30		1:30	
2:00		2:00		2:00		2:00	
2:30		2:30		2:30		2:30	
3:00		3:00		3:00		3:00	
3:30		3:30		3:30		3:30	
4:00		4:00		4:00		4:00	
4:30		4:30		4:30		4:30	
5:00		5:00		5:00		5:00	
5:30		5:30		5:30		5:30	
6:00		6:00		6:00		6:00	
6:30		6:30		6:30		6:30	
7:00		7:00		7:00		7:00	
7:30		7:30		7:30		7:30	
8:00		8:00		8:00		8:00	
WRITING PROGRESS		WRITING PROGRESS		WRITING PROGRESS		WRITING PROGRESS	

LOOKING AHEAD

Week Of

"A goal without a plan is just a wish."
—Antoine de Saint-Exupéry

PRIORITY GOALS

TO DO

DREAM GOALS

	MONDAY		TUESDAY		WEDNESDAY
	INTENTIONS		INTENTIONS		INTENTIONS
6:00		6:00		6:00	
6:30		6:30		6:30	
7:00		7:00		7:00	
7:30		7:30		7:30	
8:00		8:00		8:00	
8:30		8:30		8:30	
9:00		9:00		9:00	
9:30		9:30		9:30	
10:00		10:00		10:00	
10:30		10:30		10:30	
11:00		11:00		11:00	
11:30		11:30		11:30	
	I AM CREATIVE		MY WORDS MATTER		LIFE IS GOOD
12:00		12:00		12:00	
12:30		12:30		12:30	
1:00		1:00		1:00	
1:30		1:30		1:30	
2:00		2:00		2:00	
2:30		2:30		2:30	
3:00		3:00		3:00	
3:30		3:30		3:30	
4:00		4:00		4:00	
4:30		4:30		4:30	
5:00		5:00		5:00	
5:30		5:30		5:30	
6:00		6:00		6:00	
6:30		6:30		6:30	
7:00		7:00		7:00	
7:30		7:30		7:30	
8:00		8:00		8:00	
WRITING PROGRESS		WRITING PROGRESS		WRITING PROGRESS	
GRATITUDES					

THURSDAY		FRIDAY		SATURDAY		SUNDAY	
INTENTIONS		INTENTIONS		INTENTIONS		INTENTIONS	
6:00		6:00		6:00		6:00	
6:30		6:30		6:30		6:30	
7:00		7:00		7:00		7:00	
7:30		7:30		7:30		7:30	
8:00		8:00		8:00		8:00	
8:30		8:30		8:30		8:30	
9:00		9:00		9:00		9:00	
9:30		9:30		9:30		9:30	
10:00		10:00		10:00		10:00	
10:30		10:30		10:30		10:30	
11:00		11:00		11:00		11:00	
11:30		11:30		11:30		11:30	
	I MEET MY GOALS		BUILDING MY DREAMS		NO EXCUSES		I AM AN AUTHOR
12:00		12:00		12:00		12:00	
12:30		12:30		12:30		12:30	
1:00		1:00		1:00		1:00	
1:30		1:30		1:30		1:30	
2:00		2:00		2:00		2:00	
2:30		2:30		2:30		2:30	
3:00		3:00		3:00		3:00	
3:30		3:30		3:30		3:30	
4:00		4:00		4:00		4:00	
4:30		4:30		4:30		4:30	
5:00		5:00		5:00		5:00	
5:30		5:30		5:30		5:30	
6:00		6:00		6:00		6:00	
6:30		6:30		6:30		6:30	
7:00		7:00		7:00		7:00	
7:30		7:30		7:30		7:30	
8:00		8:00		8:00		8:00	
WRITING PROGRESS		WRITING PROGRESS		WRITING PROGRESS		WRITING PROGRESS	

LOOKING AHEAD

Week Of

Good things come to those who wait, but better things come to those who take action!

PRIORITY GOALS

TO DO

DREAM GOALS

	MONDAY	TUESDAY	WEDNESDAY
	INTENTIONS	INTENTIONS	INTENTIONS
6:00			
6:30			
7:00			
7:30			
8:00			
8:30			
9:00			
9:30			
10:00			
10:30			
11:00			
11:30			
	I AM CREATIVE	MY WORDS MATTER	LIFE IS GOOD
12:00			
12:30			
1:00			
1:30			
2:00			
2:30			
3:00			
3:30			
4:00			
4:30			
5:00			
5:30			
6:00			
6:30			
7:00			
7:30			
8:00			
WRITING PROGRESS		WRITING PROGRESS	WRITING PROGRESS
GRATITUDES			

THURSDAY		FRIDAY		SATURDAY		SUNDAY	
INTENTIONS		INTENTIONS		INTENTIONS		INTENTIONS	
6:00		6:00		6:00		6:00	
6:30		6:30		6:30		6:30	
7:00		7:00		7:00		7:00	
7:30		7:30		7:30		7:30	
8:00		8:00		8:00		8:00	
8:30		8:30		8:30		8:30	
9:00		9:00		9:00		9:00	
9:30		9:30		9:30		9:30	
10:00		10:00		10:00		10:00	
10:30		10:30		10:30		10:30	
11:00		11:00		11:00		11:00	
11:30		11:30		11:30		11:30	
	I MEET MY GOALS		BUILDING MY DREAMS		NO EXCUSES		I AM AN AUTHOR
12:00		12:00		12:00		12:00	
12:30		12:30		12:30		12:30	
1:00		1:00		1:00		1:00	
1:30		1:30		1:30		1:30	
2:00		2:00		2:00		2:00	
2:30		2:30		2:30		2:30	
3:00		3:00		3:00		3:00	
3:30		3:30		3:30		3:30	
4:00		4:00		4:00		4:00	
4:30		4:30		4:30		4:30	
5:00		5:00		5:00		5:00	
5:30		5:30		5:30		5:30	
6:00		6:00		6:00		6:00	
6:30		6:30		6:30		6:30	
7:00		7:00		7:00		7:00	
7:30		7:30		7:30		7:30	
8:00		8:00		8:00		8:00	
WRITING PROGRESS		WRITING PROGRESS		WRITING PROGRESS		WRITING PROGRESS	

LOOKING AHEAD

Week Of

"A writer only begins a book. A reader finishes it."
—Samuel Johnson

PRIORITY GOALS

TO DO

DREAM GOALS

	MONDAY		TUESDAY		WEDNESDAY
	INTENTIONS		INTENTIONS		INTENTIONS
6:00		6:00		6:00	
6:30		6:30		6:30	
7:00		7:00		7:00	
7:30		7:30		7:30	
8:00		8:00		8:00	
8:30		8:30		8:30	
9:00		9:00		9:00	
9:30		9:30		9:30	
10:00		10:00		10:00	
10:30		10:30		10:30	
11:00		11:00		11:00	
11:30		11:30		11:30	
	I AM CREATIVE		MY WORDS MATTER		LIFE IS GOOD
12:00		12:00		12:00	
12:30		12:30		12:30	
1:00		1:00		1:00	
1:30		1:30		1:30	
2:00		2:00		2:00	
2:30		2:30		2:30	
3:00		3:00		3:00	
3:30		3:30		3:30	
4:00		4:00		4:00	
4:30		4:30		4:30	
5:00		5:00		5:00	
5:30		5:30		5:30	
6:00		6:00		6:00	
6:30		6:30		6:30	
7:00		7:00		7:00	
7:30		7:30		7:30	
8:00		8:00		8:00	
WRITING PROGRESS		WRITING PROGRESS		WRITING PROGRESS	

GRATITUDES

THURSDAY		FRIDAY		SATURDAY		SUNDAY	
INTENTIONS		INTENTIONS		INTENTIONS		INTENTIONS	
6:00		6:00		6:00		6:00	
6:30		6:30		6:30		6:30	
7:00		7:00		7:00		7:00	
7:30		7:30		7:30		7:30	
8:00		8:00		8:00		8:00	
8:30		8:30		8:30		8:30	
9:00		9:00		9:00		9:00	
9:30		9:30		9:30		9:30	
10:00		10:00		10:00		10:00	
10:30		10:30		10:30		10:30	
11:00		11:00		11:00		11:00	
11:30		11:30		11:30		11:30	
	I MEET MY GOALS		BUILDING MY DREAMS		NO EXCUSES		I AM AN AUTHOR
12:00		12:00		12:00		12:00	
12:30		12:30		12:30		12:30	
1:00		1:00		1:00		1:00	
1:30		1:30		1:30		1:30	
2:00		2:00		2:00		2:00	
2:30		2:30		2:30		2:30	
3:00		3:00		3:00		3:00	
3:30		3:30		3:30		3:30	
4:00		4:00		4:00		4:00	
4:30		4:30		4:30		4:30	
5:00		5:00		5:00		5:00	
5:30		5:30		5:30		5:30	
6:00		6:00		6:00		6:00	
6:30		6:30		6:30		6:30	
7:00		7:00		7:00		7:00	
7:30		7:30		7:30		7:30	
8:00		8:00		8:00		8:00	
WRITING PROGRESS		WRITING PROGRESS		WRITING PROGRESS		WRITING PROGRESS	

LOOKING AHEAD

Month:

MONDAY	TUESDAY	WEDNESDAY

This Month's Focus

Social Media Goals

For YEAR IN REVIEW, order your next AUTHOR JOURNEY Planner Now!

Visit yotbpress.com/authorjourney

THURSDAY	FRIDAY	SATURDAY	SUNDAY

 Sales / Releases / Queries

Book List

- [x] Books in My Genre
- [ ]
- [ ]
- [ ]
- [ ]
- [ ]
- [ ]
- [ ]
- [ ]
- [ ]
- [ ]
- [ ]
- [x] Books on Business
- [ ]
- [ ]
- [ ]
- [ ]
- [ ]
- [ ]
- [ ]
- [ ]
- [ ]

Book List

☑ Books on Writing Craft

☐
☐
☐
☐
☐
☐
☐
☐
☐
☐
☐

☑ Other

☐
☐
☐
☐
☐
☐
☐
☐
☐

Need more room for your reading list?
Visit YOTBpress.com/authorjourney for free printables!

Story Ideas

Story Ideas

Need more room for your story ideas?
Visit YOTBpress.com/authorjourney for free printables!

Story Ideas

Story Ideas

Need more room for your story ideas?
Visit YOTBpress.com/authorjourney for free printables!

Resources for Writers

Obviously this list is not comprehensive, nor does it seek to be. Instead we have chosen the books and courses that unlocked something magical for us, ones that made our writing and publishing dreams possible, productive, and infinitely repeatable.

Inspiration

Big Magic—Elizabeth Gilbert

Writing Down the Bones—Natalie Goldberg

On Writing—Stephen King

Bird by Bird—Anne Lamott

The War of Art—Steven Pressfield

The Writing Process

The Emotion Thesaurus—Angela Ackerman and Becca Puglisi

Writing Active…(series)—Mary Buckham

Writing Fiction—Janet Burroway

From Where You Dream—Robert Olen Butler

Story Genius—Lisa Cron

QuickandDirtyTips.com/GrammarGirl—Mignon Fogarty (think Strunk & White, but more fun)

Story—Robert McKee

The Anatomy of Story—John Truby

Poetry

The Poetry Home Repair Manual—Ted Kooser

Children's

Writing Children's Books—Anthony D. Fredericks

Writing Picture Books—Ann Paul

Writing with Pictures—Uri Shulevitz

Institute of Children's Literature (home study course)

Audio

The Successful Author Mindset—Joanna Penn

Meditations for Mindful Writers—Dr. Madhu Wangu

Business

Self-Publishing 101 (video course)—Mark Dawson

Ads for Authors (video course)—Mark Dawson

Profit First—Michael Michalowicz

Successful Self-Publishing—Joanna Penn

Podcasts

Self-Publishing Show—Mark Dawson and James Blatch

The Creative Penn—Joanna Penn

Save time! Visit YOTBpress.com/authorjourney for a hyperlinked list of these resources.

Submission Tracker

#	Title	Word Count	Deadline	Date Submitted	Decision Notified
1.	*My Delphi*	<1500	12/15	4/30	
2.					
3.					
4.					
5.					
6.					
7.					
8.					
9.					
10.					
11.					
12.					
13.					
14.					
15.					
16.					
17.					
18.					
19.					
20.					
21.					
22.					

Submission Tracker

Publisher	Contact Info	Submission Guidelines URL

1. *Mid-American Review* — http://casit.bgsu.edu/
2.
3.
4.
5.
6.
7.
8.
9.
10.
11.
12.
13.
14.
15.
16.
17.
18.
19.
20.
21.
22.

Need more room for your submission tracker?
Visit YOTBpress.com/authorjourney for free printables!

Income

Date	Description	Amount
		$
		$
		$
		$
		$
		$
		$
		$
		$
		$
		$
		$
		$
		$
		$
		$
		$
		$
		$
		$
		$
		$

Income

Date	Description	Amount
		$
		$
		$
		$
		$
		$
		$
		$
		$
		$
		$
		$
		$
		$
		$
		$
		$
		$
		$
		$
		$
		$

Need more room for tracking your income? WAY TO GO!
Visit YOTBpress.com/authorjourney for free printables!

Expenses

Date   Description   Category

Expenses

Date Description Category

_____

_____

_____

_____

_____

_____

_____

_____

_____

_____

_____

_____

_____

_____

_____

_____

Category Key:

Capital Expenses
Business Use of Home
Business Use of Car

Travel
Entertainment
Mileage
Supplies
Postage

Professional Development
Advertising
Taxes
Rental
Cost of Goods Sold

Need more room for tracking expenses?
Visit YOTBpress.com/authorjourney for free printables!

Publishing Contacts

Name Email/Phone # Company

Publishing Contacts

Name Email/Phone # Company

About the Authors

USA Today bestselling author **LAURIE J. EDWARDS** is also a freelance editor and illustrator. In addition to having more than 2300 magazine and educational articles published, she is the author of 50+ books for children and adults in print or forthcoming under several pen names.

A former teacher and librarian, as well as the founder and former owner of Leap Books, a small YA publishing house, Laurie works as a freelance editor and/or copy editor for several educational publishers and speaks at writing conferences and events around the country. She also teaches writing classes for A Novel Idea, Story Makers, and for several universities.

After receiving an MA from Vermont College, she received her MFA in Children's Writing and Illustrating from Hollins University, and her first illustrated picture book app, *The Teeny Tiny Woman*, was picked up by RIF (Reading is Fundamental) for their Billion eBook Gift program, and 20 million copies were distributed to families around the world.

To connect with Laurie or find out more about her and her writing, visit her website, Facebook, or Twitter.

Website: www.lauriejedwards.com

Facebook: www.facebook.com/laurie.j.edwards

Twitter: https://twitter.com/lauriejedwards

Dr. DEMI STEVENS, CEO, Year of the Book press, turns writing dreams into successfully published books. She has personally assisted in the production of 350 titles by more than 150 authors, ranging from children's picture books to sizzling romance, award-winning mysteries, and bestselling business books.

She holds degrees from West Virginia University, Capital, Northwestern, and Ohio State, and has taught at Ohio State University and Delaware Valley College, and served as Director of Paul Smith Library in southcentral Pennsylvania.

Many clients call Demi the "Book Whisperer," but perhaps "Book Midwife" is more appropriate, because literary labor and delivery can be so painful. Each year she coaches a limited number of writers one-on-one through the entire drafting, editing, and publishing process.

To learn more, visit: YOTBpress.com

Or email her at: demi@yotbpress.com

Let's make this YOUR Year of the Book!

Notes

Notes

Notes

Notes

Notes

www.ingramcontent.com/pod-product-compliance
Lightning Source LLC
Chambersburg PA
CBHW081228080526
44587CB00022B/3866